CHIPPEWA FAMILIES

CHIPPEWA FAMILIES

A Social Study of
White Earth Reservation, 1938

SISTER M. INEZ HILGER

with a new introduction by
BRENDA J. CHILD
and
KIMBERLY M. BLAESER

MINNESOTA HISTORICAL SOCIETY PRESS
St. Paul

Borealis Books are high-quality paperback reprints of books chosen by the Minnesota Historical Society Press for their importance as enduring historical sources and their value as enjoyable accounts of life in the Upper Midwest.

Cover: *Indian Education,* by Patrick DesJarlait, 1970, watercolor on paper, collection of the Minnesota Historical Society

♾ The paper used in this publication meets the minimum requirements of the American National Standard for Information Sciences–Permanence for Printed Library Materials, ANSI Z39.48–1984.

Minnesota Historical Society Press, St. Paul

© 1939 by the Catholic University of America Press
New material © 1998 by the Minnesota Historical Society

International Standard Book Number 0-87351-352-5
Manufactured in the United States of America

10 9 8 7 6 5 4 3 2 1

Library of Congress Cataloging-in-Publication Data

Hilger, M. Inez (Mary Inez), 1891–
    Chippewa families : a social study of White Earth Reservation, 1938 / M. Inez Hilger ; with a new introduction by Brenda J. Child and Kimberly M. Blaeser.
        p. cm.
    Originally published: Washington, D.C. : Catholic University of America Press, 1939.
    Includes bibliographical references and index.
    ISBN 0-87351-352-5 (paperback : alk. paper)
    1. Ojibwa Indians–Social conditions. 2. White Earth Indian Reservation (Minn.) 3. Ojibwa Indians–Housing. I. Title.
E99.C6H464
305.89730776–dc21   97-42937

TABLE OF CONTENTS

Introduction to the Reprint Edition

OJIBWAY COUNTRY, 1938

A decade before anthropologist M. Inez Hilger began research for *Chippewa Families: A Social Study of White Earth Reservation, 1938,* historian William Watts Folwell completed the fourth and final volume of his significant monograph, *A History of Minnesota.*[1] In a remarkable chapter entitled "The Tragedy of White Earth," Folwell described the Nelson Act of 1889 and the national allotment policy, which attempted to establish private ownership of communally held tribal land for the "benefit" of American Indians in need of "civilization." Historians have estimated that American Indians across the United States were deprived of two-thirds of their total remaining land base during the allotment era (1887–1934). Folwell's account, undoubtedly read by Hilger, outlined in unforgettable detail a history of the corruption and tribal dispossession that unfolded in northern Minnesota after 1889.

White Earth Reservation had been created by treaty in 1867 as the reservation for the Mississippi, Gull Lake, Pembina, and Otter Tail Pillager bands of Ojibway. It was distinguished for its diversity of prairies, lakes, and forests. But the frenzy for tribal real estate on the part of the federal government, state politicians, local banks and residents, and the regional pine cartel left the Ojibway of White Earth nearly landless.[2] Land fraud perpetrated upon Native people was rampant, and the inter-

1. William Watts Folwell, *A History of Minnesota* (St. Paul: Minnesota Historical Society, 1930, 1969), 4:261–83; see also p. 283–96. Hilger's research project became her doctoral dissertation and was published as *A Social Study of One Hundred Fifty Chippewa Indian Families of the White Earth Reservation of Minnesota* (Washington, D.C.: Catholic University of America Press, 1939). The various tribal names in use include Chippewa, Ojibway, Ojibwe, Ojibwa, Anishinabe, and Anishinaabe.

2. More recent documentations of the White Earth dispossession have been published. See Melissa L. Meyer, *The White Earth Tragedy: Ethnicity and Dispossession at a Minnesota*

ests of ecocidal timber companies dominated the political landscape of the western Great Lakes region.

The consequences of this immense exploitation of people, land, and resources resonated at White Earth for many years. Out-migrations from White Earth, increased participation in wage labor, and a continued degradation of wild-rice stands and other environments contributed to a deterioration of the traditional Ojibway seasonal economy. Tribal members worked at a number of off-reservation odd jobs, and many people found new sources of income in farming or in the lumber industry in Minnesota, while another part of the community departed to new work and new lives in Fargo or Minneapolis and St. Paul. Land loss at White Earth and other reservations was the catalyst for a shift in population away from the rural location and to urban centers. Newly established patterns of mobility accelerated during the Great Depression of the 1930s and World War II.[3]

The families that Hilger encountered at White Earth and other Ojibway reservations during the 1930s were the survivors of removals, resource exploitation, deception, land loss, economic decline, and disease. They had also been the targets of federal policies designed to destroy culture and rupture family and tribal ties. The changes wrought during the preceding fifty years had been monumental, more complex than Hilger understood when she contemplated the relationship between housing and Ojibway social problems and beliefs. The once

Anishinaabe Reservation, 1889–1920 (Lincoln: University of Nebraska Press, 1994), and Holly YoungBear-Tibbetts, "Without Due Process: The Alienation of Individual Trust Allotments of the White Earth Anishinaabeg," *American Indian Culture and Research Journal* 15 (Special Edition: The Political Geography of Indian Country, 1991): 93–138.

3. For an excellent source of information about economic change and the role of wild rice in the cultural life of Great Lakes Ojibway people, see Thomas Vennum, Jr., *Wild Rice and the Ojibway People* (St. Paul: Minnesota Historical Society Press, 1988). Two fine autobiographies document the movement of Ojibway families from northern Minnesota to Minneapolis. Ignatia Broker worked in a defense plant in the Twin Cities during World War II and wrote about the discrimination in employment and housing she and other American Indian people faced in the urban setting. She later wrote *Night Flying Woman: An Ojibway Narrative* (St. Paul: Minnesota Historical Society Press, 1983). Gerald Vizenor's family left White Earth during the depression, moving first to Detroit Lakes, Minnesota, and then to Minneapolis, where Vizenor was born in 1934. His touching autobiography is *Interior Landscapes: Autobiographical Myths and Metaphors* (Minneapolis: University of Minnesota Press, 1990).

stately pine trees had been cleared from White Earth by timber companies. The land base had declined by 90 percent, and new Euro-American
landowners, beneficiaries of tribal losses, populated northern Minnesota.

The larger community at White Earth in 1938, as Hilger noted, was
characterized by a broadening cultural diversity. In fact, she decided
against interviewing "Chippewa families so situated economically and
socially that they were distinguishable from whites only with some difficulty," even though the families were enrolled at White Earth (p. xxii).
The populace was not homogeneous and often contested issues con-
cerning acculturation, language preference, and spiritual belief. Métis
families had long formed a significant group on the reservation, took an
active role in the politics and events, and early in the century maintained
large households with numerous children.

Ojibway families, sometimes described as "conservative" by historians, tended to have fewer children, but the census of 1910 listed many
individuals as "dependents" within households.[4] An increase in the number of extended households at White Earth after 1910 was another result
of economic decline generated by the land fraud. Class differences
became more pronounced, and rural poverty contributed to an enduring rift in tribal politics. The old Ojibway economy, with seasonal rounds
of hunting, fishing, making maple sugar, harvesting fruits and wild rice,
was restricted by a diminished land base but remained crucial to reservation subsistence and Ojibway identity at White Earth and other twen-
tieth-century communities.

Poverty, diaspora, and disease continued to influence family life at
White Earth in the early twentieth century. Deaths from pulmonary diseases and influenza escalated. Surveys conducted during the 1930s
revealed alarmingly high rates of tuberculosis among Indians in
Minnesota, estimated to be as high as 15 percent among the Native population.[5] Some residents at White Earth were also plagued by trachoma,
a highly contagious eye disease that was not a medical problem for the
majority population in the United States.

Ojibway families historically responded with generosity to family
members and the community at large during seasons of crisis. When the

4. Frederick E. Hoxie, Richard A. Sattler, and Nancy Shoemaker, *Reports of the American
Indian Family History Project,* Occasional Papers Series, The Newberry Library Center for
the History of the American Indian (Chicago: Newberry Library, 1992), 28–30.
5. For a discussion of epidemic disease in Wisconsin and Minnesota Ojibway communities, see Edmund Jefferson Danziger, Jr., *The Chippewas of Lake Superior* (Norman:
University of Oklahoma Press, 1978), 110–33.

Great Depression penetrated Indian country, alienation from land, loss of wages, and the presence of terrible communicable diseases merged with profound social problems at White Earth. Time-honored methods of caring for the needy and adopting parentless children proved to be inadequate. One sign of the strain on the social fabric was the growing number of Indian children applying to and attending government boarding schools. Some of these children were orphans, some had been trying to raise younger siblings on their own, and others came from intact families devastated by economic hard times. High enrollments reflected the dreadful state of reservation economies and the barriers to stable family life during the 1930s. The schools were the only remaining source of adequate food, shelter, and clothing.[6]

Since their inception boarding schools had been a reservoir of bitter acrimony that strained a relationship between American Indian families and the federal government, which was already characterized by distrust. In the midwestern states, schools were seldom located in areas close to Indian communities, making the transition from home to institution traumatic for children. When the schools were designed during the allotment era, assimilationist reformers argued that the task of "civilizing" Indian children would be easier and lapses into tribal ways less likely if students stayed away from their homes and relatives until their education was complete. The shortcomings of boarding schools were legendary within the Indian community. Hilger found the lack of enthusiasm for schooling among her informants somewhat of a mystery. Trained as an anthropologist and a Benedictine sister in the Roman Catholic church, Hilger wrote, "One wonders why twenty-one per cent on the reservation should be illiterate when such fine opportunities for education had been offered them," including the "mission schools" (p. 77).

Ojibway children continued to attend mission and federal boarding schools in the 1930s, even though the popularity of the residential school concept had withered in the eyes of progressive reformers.[7] Many schools were closed when John Collier, a passionate critic of the boarding schools, became commissioner of Indian affairs in 1933. A dozen boarding schools had already closed in the United States between 1928 and 1933, but the number of Indian students attending residential

6. Brenda J. Child, *Boarding School Seasons: American Indian Families, 1900–1940* (Lincoln: University of Nebraska Press, forthcoming).

7. Frederick E. Hoxie, *A Final Promise: The Campaign to Assimilate the Indians, 1880–1920* (Lincoln: University of Nebraska Press, 1984), 202–10.

schools increased. When the deprivation of Indian families became acute during the 1930s, the boarding schools filled with students. Depression-era records from the Red Lake Reservation in northern Minnesota recorded a truckload of hungry children arriving from White Earth to be placed in their boarding school because their own families were unable to provide for them.[8] Ojibway children along with the adults suffered the repercussions of economic depression.

In one case, which occurred during the summer of 1939, a White Earth teenager named Wallace transferred from a boarding school in North Dakota to the Flandreau Institute in South Dakota. Since the age of six, Wallace's only home had been a government boarding school. Wallace's widowed mother, unable to cope any longer with her financial burden and corresponding household instability, sent him and his five siblings away to school. Wallace did not return to White Earth; instead he lived his entire childhood and adolescence in government boarding schools before entering the army at the age of nineteen.[9]

White Earth families told how they survived hard times during the depression. A mother and father from Mahnomen sent two sons to boarding school at Flandreau and a daughter to Haskell Institute in Kansas in the 1930s. Not long after parting from their children, the parents wrote anguished letters to school administrators, distressed by having to separate their children between schools and not convinced they had made the right decision. Their eighty-acre farm in rural Mahnomen with only a two-room house had proved to be inadequate for an extended household of thirteen family members, and their children were missing long stretches of school during northern Minnesota's hard winters of heavy snowfall.[10]

In 1933 a man from the St. Croix Ojibway community of Wisconsin remembered a better time for his people, when the seasonal round had nourished the Ojibway, and made the observation that "when they were children an Indian family was never without meat or fruit as is now the case."[11] American Indian families in the western Great Lakes area found some relief from hardship during the depression through emergency government programs, such as the Works Project Administration (WPA)

8. Miscellaneous correspondence, Red Lake Boarding School Papers, Red Lake Tribal Archives, Red Lake, Minnesota.

9. Bureau of Indian Affairs (BIA), Application for admission to non-reservation school form, Flandreau Student File, June 28, 1939, National Archives, Record Group 75.

10. BIA, Flandreau Student File, 1931, NARG 75.

11. BIA, Flandreau miscellaneous correspondence, undated, NARG 75.

and the Indian Division of the Civilian Conservation Corps (CCC–ID). Hilger pointed out the nearly universal reliance on poverty relief and pension programs at White Earth in 1938. Of the 150 families in her study, "one hundred forty-eight were drawing U.S. Government checks of either W.P.A., C.C.C.–I.D., World War veterans' pensions, Social Security Act, or I.S. Division of Roads' funds" (p. 131).

As with other Americans, the Ojibway weathered the worst miseries of the depression through hard work and active participation in poverty-relief programs. American Indians constructed dams, built roads to secluded areas, worked on housing projects, and watched for forest fires in the wooded regions of northern states. The Bureau of Indian Affairs employed Indian office workers through the WPA. Parents joined their children in education programs sponsored by the WPA to advance English reading and writing skills. To their credit, families persisted in the aftermath of a massive land grab, dealt with a great inequality of resources, and survived the worst economic depression the United States had ever endured.

Hilger's fieldwork and study of family life, housing, and Ojibway society left unexamined a longer history that continued to influence the White Earth community in 1938.[12] Hilger no doubt underestimated many strengths of the Ojibway people, believing she had observed two sorts of persons. One group she imagined "contented," living in tar-paper shacks on the reservation, secure in their government hand-outs, and limited to "a subsistence standard" (p. 147). A larger, second group she conceived of as more enterprising, "willing to be shown how they may assist themselves," with a preference for dwelling in superior frame-style houses. In some ways her comments appear to resemble those older stereotypes of "indolent" and "lazy" Indians or modern condemnations of welfare recipients for "a simple lack of motivation." But Hilger's analysis was more sophisticated. She recognized that White Earth was a community in transition—and one still strongly influenced by Ojibway traditional culture.

By 1938 the Ojibway families of White Earth had experienced fifty years of devastating loss, tremendous cultural change, a damaging educational policy, and a descent into economic depression. Their future was uncertain. Following the adoption of a tribal constitution in 1936, White Earth underwent governmental restructuring as part of the

12. For an excellent interpretation of Hilger's work, see Jean M. O'Brien, "Introduction to the Reprint Edition," in M. Inez Hilger, *Chippewa Child Life and Its Cultural Background* (St. Paul: Minnesota Historical Society Press, Borealis Books, 1992).

Minnesota Chippewa Tribe. Still to come were the challenges of World War II, new federal programs for relocating more of their population in cities, intense tribal politics, a long legal struggle for compensation for loss of and restoration of land, and the advent of a new gaming operation. Their survival as an Ojibway community with a complicated history, part rural reservation and part urban, is a tribute to their own resilience and creativity.

BRENDA J. CHILD

Red Lake Chippewa
University of Minnesota

During five or six months of 1938, between June and November, Mary Inez Hilger, a sister from the Order of St. Benedict, lived on the White Earth Reservation in northwestern Minnesota and gathered facts about housing structures and living conditions of Indian families residing there. Her research, commissioned by the Bureau of Indian Affairs, was a part of a larger effort to gather survey material about each of the seven Ojibway reservations in Minnesota. Hilger subsequently used the field-work to write her dissertation and complete her doctoral degree in social science at the Catholic University in Washington, D.C. She supple-mented the information she gathered during her time at White Earth with notes from her previous ethnological research among the Minnesota Ojibway of Red Lake Reservation in the summers of 1932 and 1933 and among the Wisconsin and Michigan Ojibway of Lac Courte Oreille, Lac du Flambeau, La Pointe, and L'Anse Reservations in the summer of 1935. This reprint of her dissertation, first published in 1939 as *A Social Study of One Hundred Fifty Chippewa Indian Families of the White Earth Reservation of Minnesota,* offers the reader several angles from which to gain an understanding of the world of the Anishinaabe in the late 1930s.

First, there is the wealth of material Hilger gathered that summer of 1938 regarding housing, living conditions, and social status at White Earth. The information she compiled not only detailed structural aspects of housing, such as type of building, materials used in construction, number and size of rooms, types of doors, windows, and heating units, but offered an unusual accounting of day-to-day living matters, check-ing water sources, assessing produce production and storage, detailing methods of doing laundry, describing preservation methods for meat and fish, and enumerating household equipment, from bedding to towels to tableware. Hilger not only counted the number of occupants and cal-culated cubic feet of living space per person, but she recorded details about each individual's education, livelihood, travel experiences, religious affiliations, and participation in "traditional" Native activities like ricing or beading. The tabulated results of Hilger's investigation are a rich resource for anyone wanting specifics; they stand as a concrete catalog of material culture.

But the text includes story as well as itemization. Hilger explored per-sonal areas, such as retention of the Ojibway language, marital status, and alcohol consumption. She compared "legitimate" and "illegitimate" birth patterns. She recorded statements by her informants evaluating different community reputations. The material in the study includes the voices and views of several members of the White Earth Nation in 1938. We can read the personal as well as the statistical.

Another view this reprint offers is one unplanned by the author. Hilger's approach to the fieldwork–her perspectives, assumptions, and conclusions–convey a great deal about the culture and the era of 1930s America from which this study emerged. What counted in the counting, what possessions were thought to reveal in their presence or absence about individuals or family units, what questions were asked and how they were stated, what relationships were inferred between living standards and morality–these things disclose as much about the compiler and her social history as they do about the subjects of the inquiry. They expose a certain bias, uncover stereotypical views, and reflect a particular cultural stance in regard to the study and further "civilization" of American Indian people.

Read from these many angles, Hilger's *Chippewa Families* is a rich and fascinating document, one that supplies abundant raw data, incorporates personal commentary on the data from two different cultures, and becomes a kind of character analysis of social anthropology of the 1930s. Finally, Hilger's observations of and suggestions regarding labor, law enforcement, and educational programs offer another historical view of the making and implementation of policies affecting Indian nations.

The layers of story available in Hilger's study can be seen clearly, for example, in an examination of her primary consideration: selection of the sample group of families. Although the presentation of her findings is titled a "social study" of Ojibway families, Hilger's work had its basis in an assessment of housing structures and her attempt to determine to what degree living conditions dictated intangibles, such as personal aspirations, spiritual expression, or social problems. Hilger's sample, then, was created to include a range of physical structures. She reported that her selections were made "with the advice of white persons who had been in the service of the White Earth Indians for some years and who themselves had visited the homes in the various localities." These selections were next "discussed with some intelligent and reliable Indian, a resident in the locality, to make certain that they were a cross-section, economically, socially, and morally, of his community" (p. xxii).

Although Hilger's description of her process was undoubtedly meant to establish the credibility of her findings, read almost sixty years later, it acts instead as a signal for caution, reminding the reader to evaluate the context of the information presented as well as the circumstances of its compilation. Her decision to use "white persons" in making her selections essentially introduced a step of cultural translation and created a distance from her primary sources, a distortion that must be accounted for in a review of the results. Who, we might ask today, would know more about Ojibway housing patterns than Ojibway Indians themselves?

Hilger's language itself reveals certain personal or cultural bias. In this instance, for example, the presumption of superior understanding on the part of the whites inherent in Hilger's procedure is reinforced by her statements about that procedure. Her perspective becomes clearer and her bias more overt with her reference to some "intelligent and reliable" Indian. The "white persons" required no such characterization and were apparently assumed to be both intelligent and reliable by race or background, but the Indian who had these qualities was distinguished for them.

These kinds of statements and presumptions do not by any means disqualify the data collected nor necessarily undermine the conclusions. The astute reader will work to read through any distortions just as researchers have always taken time to decipher the blemished scripts of original texts and judge their importance. Indeed, because Hilger was not reluctant to insert her opinions or to speak from her Christian or assimilationist point of view, we can piece together fairly well her political and religious perspectives. And, if we are cautious not to replicate bad anthropological practices that assume the whole on the basis of the part, we have a valuable sample of one operative element or at least one strain of thinking about Indians in postallotment America.

An analysis of Hilger's selection procedure must also evaluate both her determination that certain Indian communities were not greatly distinguishable from those of whites and her decision therefore to exclude those areas from the sample. Contemporary Anishinaabe who resided in several of these communities during the time of Hilger's research disagreed with her assessment of the living conditions of that era as being on a par with that of their white neighbors. Even were Hilger's appraisal taken to be accurate, the exclusion of that supposedly more prosperous segment of the population would create flawed results.

Perhaps Hilger's decision arose from a philosophical allegiance to a belief in "pure" culture. Her logic for excluding the families she saw as "economically and socially" less distinguishable from the whites was that they would "distort the picture of *what is generally known as the people of the White Earth Reservation*" (p. xxii, emphasis added). If we place this comment in the context of Hilger's categorizing and characterizing of her subjects by generations, her emphasis on such things as first language and language retention and participation in cultural practices like weaving and the use of herbal medicine, her claim of a clear relationship between generational positioning and drinking, marital practices, and even degree of contentedness, and her rhetoric about "traditional tribal customs," "primitive culture," "the old culture," and "old Chippewa ways," we uncover a pattern of measurement that stems from a philosophical vision of a static culture. The "real Chippewa," Hilger apparently believed, were not those whose economic situation approached parity with white neighbors or who had in the most tangible ways adapted to or incorporated aspects of white culture.

In fact, throughout the presentation of her investigation, Hilger seemed troubled that the conditions she found did not align with either her Christian standard or her ideal of "the old culture." Here it is possible to read one of the several interesting subtexts of the study. When reporting on the continued existence of the Midē wiwin, the Ojibway Grand Medicine or religious society, for instance, Hilger noted: "After reading Hoffman's description of the Midē wiwin one is led to believe, however, that the ceremonials on the White Earth Reservation are losing much of their earlier interest and exactness" (p. 82). She reported on alterations in the construction of the lodge, the lack of face paint on some of the participants, and how nonmembers who visited the grounds during ceremonies were "listening to a radio announcement of a baseball game" or "visiting in the shade" while "children played noisily" (p. 82–83). Those changes and activities apparently violated her image of proper "old time" ceremony.

Although the older Ojibway ways were not viewed by Hilger as totally acceptable or as "advanced" as those of her own religion or civilization, she appeared to find in them a certain nobility and believed they offered a solid social structure she found lacking on the 1938 White Earth Reservation. Whereas Hilger portrayed the precontact Ojibway as "a roaming people of no formal education" and "a people who had not yet advanced beyond the stage of hunting and food gathering," she acknowledged that they had a "distinct, well-established, and well-integrated culture" (p. 4). But, she claimed, the government attempt at forced assimilation "has done something to them spiritually" (p. 4). Hilger described the changes most frequently with a rhetoric of loss: "From an independent and distinctive people, they have become one lacking initiative, incentive, enthusiasm, independence, self-respect" (p. 4).

Hilger voiced strong disapproval, even at times distaste, for the lifestyles she encountered as she undertook visits to the various reservation families. Particularly revealing are her assessments of the different villages or communities represented in the study and the kind of class system she sketched. When writing about White Earth village, for example, she pictured it as in a kind of cultural limbo: "It appeared as though social controls of the old Chippewa culture had gone out of the community and none had replaced them. It was difficult to think of White Earth village as a community of Indians; it was pathetic to think of it as one of whites!" (p. 18). In contrast she described Ponsford, a place where "Old Chippewa customs still existed" and a village that had "a larger per cent of near full bloods than any other on the reservation," as "somewhat better morally than White Earth" with occupants who were "serene and contented," and she pictured Rice Lake, Pine Bend, and Island Lake as "a contented group, little tainted by the vices of European civilization" (p. 18, 19). While Hilger clearly disapproved of the "lost" generations of Ojibway, which she believed lacked clear cultural standards, she showed tolerance for those of the older generations, even expressed a degree of admiration and compassion, but her true approval was reserved for those few civilized Christian Ojibway she encountered, those to whom she applied labels like "an outstanding Indian" (p. 65).

Hilger's moral censure of the new generations of mixed culture on White Earth Reservation is perhaps most apparent in her discussions of marriage, illegitimate children, and alcohol consumption. The marriage patterns on the reservation particularly disturbed Hilger. She devoted more than fourteen pages to their analysis, including case descriptions and statements by those interviewed. She finally voiced her frustration with the patterns of common-law marriage, separation without legal divorce, and what she called "public concubinage," labeling them as "annoying and confusing to those out of the group" (p. 66). In her moral evaluation Hilger established several separate standards, advocating a different rule for each of the different generations or categories of Indian people. In regard to common-law marriage, she was willing to support a laissez-faire policy for those "of the older generation, members of the Midē wiwin, who have lived happily in common-law marriages for years and who are in good faith" but encouraged legal enforcement of state laws regarding marriage for those of the younger second or third generations (p. 63).

To what degree Hilger's investment in her own vocation led to her preoccupation with this subject is uncertain, but the text leaves little doubt that marriage arrangements were of great consequence to the author. Her strong statements about the subject also tend to reveal her own biases, both religious and cultural. In discussing marriage between the Indian and non-Indian races, for instance, Hilger expressed astonishment that a white person would marry a Native American for reasons other than material gain. She acknowledged that Indian women perhaps would marry white men because of the possibility of enjoying a more prosperous life-style and the expectation that their children would have a social advantage, recognized that white men might marry Indian women for the sake of their and their children's annuities, but proclaimed in disbelief: "Why white women marry Indian men was not known; some thought it must be solely for love!" (p. 68).

But as humorous as some of Hilger's statements seem today, as clearly as they might expose bias to an audience reading at the end of the twentieth century, they also reveal concern for and a desire to improve the living standards of Native people, standards Hilger saw as grossly substandard. Among the important layers of story contained in *Chippewa Families* is the raw assessment of housing facts and living conditions. Hilger was frank in her appraisal of the situation she found among the 150 families of the survey, calling them "a poverty-stricken group who lived in inadequate houses and in an inadequate environment" (p. 147). The study will remain invaluable for the compilation of data, detailed physical descriptions, and sample photos that support this assessment. Hilger supplied the information in both narrative and graphic form. The astonishing range of material she was able to gather includes physical description of the dwelling and details involving ownership of both the land and the house. She described almost every aspect of daily living and provided a significant itemization of goods owned and used in the homes. In addition, Hilger pressed her informants for much personal information, which she tabulated for the study. This graphic presentation she supplemented with selected quotations from the informants.

Hilger's inclusion of comments from the residents of the wigwams, tar-paper shacks, frame houses, and rehabilitation houses, whose structure and contents she detailed so thoroughly, greatly enriches this study. The housing history of the White Earth Ojibway, Hilger realized, is not only a story of buildings but also one of those who built, inhabited, and, yes, loved those houses. A home, as Hilger defined it in the study, was "a dwelling where members of a family have a feeling of belonging, a feeling of security; where they exchange affections, sympathy, and kindness" (p. 31). When asked if she would like to leave her home, one of Hilger's informants, a fifty-year-old woman living in a tar-paper shack, answered, "My husband was born right here and I have lived here with him and my children fifteen years. I'm well acquainted with all the woods and everything out here, and I wouldn't want to move" (p. 50). As buildings,

Hilger informed us, the houses of this study met hardly any of the standards set in 1935 by the National Association of Housing Officials. But as homes, the underlying text seems to tell us, they provided a sense of connection to history, place, and family, a connection that typified as much as housing structures the social conditions of the 1938 White Earth Reservation.

KIMBERLY M. BLAESER

White Earth Chippewa
University of Wisconsin-Milwaukee

FOR FURTHER READING

Densmore, Frances. *Chippewa Customs*. Washington, D.C.: Bureau of American Ethnology Bulletin 86, Smithsonian Institution, 1929; St. Paul: Minnesota Historical Society Press, Borealis Books, 1979.

Hilger, M. Inez. *Chippewa Child Life and Its Cultural Background*. Washington, D.C.: Bureau of American Ethnology Bulletin 146, Smithsonian Institution, 1951; St. Paul: Minnesota Historical Society Press, Borealis Books, 1992.

Meyer, Melissa L. *The White Earth Tragedy: Ethnicity and Dispossession at a Minnesota Anishinaabe Reservation, 1889–1920*. Lincoln: University of Nebraska Press, 1994.

Vizenor, Gerald. *The People Named the Chippewa: Narrative Histories*. Minneapolis: University of Minnesota Press, 1984.

Preface

The purpose of this investigation, made in the summer of 1938, was to study one hundred fifty Chippewa Indian families to discover whether there was any significant relationship between the social status of the families and their housing and living conditions. The ancestors of the group studied, but four generations ago, lived in a cultural environment and followed a culture pattern decidedly different from that of Europeans who were filtering into their lands. Today their descendents are accepted by the state of Minnesota as citizens on a par with its citizens of European ancestry.

This study was undertaken to answer the following questions: In what types of houses do the Chippewa live? Is there any relationship between the type of house and the aspirations, social problems, and spiritual expressions of the family living in it? Between the type of house and the living conditions of the family residing there? The aim of this study was to answer these questions as adequately as any sample can.

A short historical summary is given in the Introduction. It is an account of the origin of the Chippewa, of a period of treaties which eventually brought them wardship under the Federal Government, of their later emancipation, and of their final acceptance as citizens of the United States.

Chapters I and II are included in order that the presence, or non-existence, of certain factors found in the analysis of the housing and living conditions of the one hundred fifty families may be better understood. The former gives the physical environment and the population basis of the White Earth Reservation; the latter, the economic, political, health, religious, educational and social opportunities of the people residing there.

Chapters III, IV, and V are an answer to the questions set at the beginning of the study. Information upon which the analysis was based was gathered while in residence on the White Earth Reservation during the months of June to November of 1938. One or both parents of the one hundred fifty families were interviewed in their own homes. Every room in all homes but two was surveyed and an ample schedule filled in with the aid of household members. (See Appendix A.) Answers regarding aspirations of the family came to light during social visits; and those to social problems, in a discussion of the possible solution of problems existing on the reservation.

The schedule was the result of a five-week preliminary survey spent in intimate contact with thirty families scattered among the various communities on the reservation. The thirty families of the preliminary study, as well as the final one hundred fifty, were chosen with the advice of white persons who had been in the service of the White Earth Indians for some years and who themselves had visited the homes in the various localities. The families so selected were then discussed with some intelligent and reliable Indian, a resident in the locality, to make certain that they were a cross-section, economically, socially, and morally, of his community.

It was discovered early in the survey that in the communities of White Earth and Naytahwaush, and in the towns on the state highway, namely Mahnomen, Bijou, Waubun, Ogema, and Callaway, there were Chippewa families so situated economically and socially that they were distinguishable from whites only with some difficulty. It was thought best not to include these in the one hundred fifty families since they would weight the final summaries so as to distort the picture of what is generally known as the people of the White Earth Reservation. They would fit more properly into a study of Chippewa who live in white communities, and who have severed connections with the White Earth Reservation excepting that of being on its roll, for annuity purposes.

Since the traditional economic, social, and moral heritage of the families was found, in the preliminary survey, to be a factor in the life of the families, it was thought well to include their cultural background. Ethnological material, therefore, was included in Chapters III, IV, and V. When no special references to sources are given, the material was gleaned from the writer's unpublished notes of ethnological research among the Chippewa on the Red Lake Reservation of Minnesota in the summers of 1932 and 1933, and on the Lac Courte Orielle, the Lac du Flambeau, and the La Pointe reservations of Wisconsin and the L'Anse Reservation of Michigan in the summer of 1935.

Special acknowledgments are due many persons for the content of this study. Especially among them is Dr. Louis Balsam, field representative of Commissioner John Collier of the U.S. Bureau of Indian Affairs, Washington, D.C., and, until recently, superintendent of the Consolidated Chippewa Agency, Duluth, Minnesota, at whose request the study was made, for his fine spirit of sympathy and helpfulness; and to

Dr. F. Stuart Chapin and Dr. Wilson D. Wallis, both of the University of Minnesota, for recommending me for the study.

Special thanks are due Mr. Melvin Hunt, assistant to the superintendent of the Consolidated Chippewa Agency, located on the White Earth Reservation, for his generous and unfailing assistance and advice; to his son, Milo, for his continuous and prompt service as chauffeur on the many field trips; to Mr. C. B. Vaughan, head of division of roads, Indian Service, Duluth, and to his staff, for preparing the maps found in the study; to my sister, Sister Marie Hilger, O.S.B., to Sister Immacula Roeder, O.S.B., and Sister Cortona Justen, O.S.B., for their splendid assistance in field work and tabulations.

I wish, too, to express my appreciation to staff members of the Consolidated Chippewa Agency, Duluth, and to the field workers on the White Earth Reservation of both the United States Indian Service and of the state of Minnesota.

My heartiest thanks are due to Mother Rosamond Praetchner, O.S.B., for her constant encouragement and interest; to Father Justine Leutmer, O.S.B., and to the Benedictine Sisters of St. Benedict's Mission, White Earth, for their hospitality during nearly the entire period of the study; to the Sisters of other Chippewa reservations for hospitality during the summers of ethnological research.

To Mr. Roy P. Wilcox of Eau Claire, Wisconsin, I owe my sincerest expression of gratitude for his unfailing interest, and for financial assistance in the field work and in the publication of this study as well as in the ethnological research among the Chippewa of Wisconsin and Michigan. To my parents, Mr. and Mrs. F. W. Hilger, and to my brothers, William and James, I wish to express my warmest appreciation for financial assistance in my ethnological research among the Chippewa of Minnesota.

To Mrs. Peter Lelonek of Altoona, Wisconsin, I owe a very special debt of gratitude for her continuous helpfulness in typing notes and manuscripts.

I especially want to express my sincere appreciation to the many Indians of the White Earth Reservation who assisted so courteously and spontaneously in the summer of 1938 in giving detailed information regarding themselves, their families, and their housing and living conditions, knowing that they had nothing to gain thereby. To the many Chippewa friends of other reservations, I express my sincere appreciation for their fine spirit of cooperation in recording "old Chippewa ways."

I also wish to express my sincere thanks to Dr. Percy Robert and Dr. Mary Elizabeth Walsh of Catholic University for reading and criticizing the study. To Dr. Paul Hanly Furfey, head of the department of sociology, Catholic University, I am deeply grateful for his guidance in making the study and for his advice, suggestions, and criticisms.

I wish to take this occasion also to thank Dr. Roy Deferrari, chairman of the Committee on Fellowships and Scholarships of the Catholic University, as well as the members of his Committee, for awarding me with the Anna Hope Hudson Scholarship for 1936–1937 and 1937–1958; and Mr. Roy P. Wilcox for his generous financial assistance, other than the scholarship, needed for the years of graduate study for the Doctor of Philosophy degree.

SISTER M. INEZ HILGER

Introduction

THE WHITE EARTH CHIPPEWA—A SHORT SKETCH

The Chippewa Indians—the name being a popular adaptation of Ojibway—belong, culturally, to the tribes of the woodland area of North America. Linguistically, they belong to the Algonquian family along with other woodland tribes, among them the Ottawa, the Sac and Fox, the Potawatomi, the Illinois, the Cree, and three tribes of the plains area, namely the Blackfoot, the Arapaho, and the Cheyenne.[1]

PLACE OF ORIGIN, EARLY HABITAT, AND PRESENT LOCATION

The place of origin of the Chippewa is not known. They have an ancient tradition that they came from the West, and many bands bury their dead facing the West, the direction, contemporary Chippewa say, in which they were journeying in returning to their own land when the white man first met them.[2]

When the white man first met them, the Chippewa occupied practically the central portion of the North American continent having come there, according to their traditions, from the shores of the Atlantic about the Gulf of the St. Lawrence.[3] Skinner describes the territory over which the Chippewa at one time roamed as extending "from the Niagara River on the east to the neighborhood of Central Montana on the west, and from the northern part of Wisconsin and Michigan north about half way to Hudson's bay."[4] Hodge notes that they came from some point north or northeast of Mackinaw.[5]

The Jesuit Relations of 1641 contain the first written word on record regarding the Chippewa, Fathers Isaac Jogues and Charles Raymbault having visited the tribe that year. In 1667, Father Allouez visited them and wrote: "They are called Sauteurs by the French because their abode is the sault by which Lake Tracy empties into the Lake of the Hurons. They speak the common Algonquin, and are easily understood."[6] Perrot found them living south of Lake Superior in 1670-99.[7]

In about 1670, the Chippewa came into possession of firearms and their westward movement was greatly aided. By the beginning of the eighteenth century, the Sioux, their greatest rivals for land occupancy, had been driven south to the Minnesota River and westward as far as the Turtle Mountains.[8]

By 1850, the Chippewa in the United States occupied "the Northern part of Michigan, or the South shore of Lake Huron; the whole Northern portion of Wisconsin Territory; all the South shore of Lake Superior, for eight hundred miles; the upper part of the Mississippi, the Sandy, Leach, and Red Lakes."[9]

Today the Chippewa of the United States are living on reservations within their original territories of Minnesota, Wisconsin, Michigan, and North Dakota. The bands in Canada are found in Ontario, Manitoba, and the North-West Territories. The entire population in both the United States and Canada in 1905 was estimated to be between thirty thousand and thirty-two thousand.[10]

TREATIES WITH THE U.S. GOVERNMENT, EXECUTIVE ORDERS,
ACTS OF CONGRESS

Treaties with the United States Government, executive orders of presidents, and special acts of Congress affecting the Chippewa tribe as a whole, and, later the various bands now found in Minnesota, began to be made as early as 1785, and have continued to be made until very recent times. Twenty-two such negotiations were made in the sixty years between 1805 and 1864.[11]

Until the nineties the Indians were continuously ceding lands while the United States Government was depositing sums of money for them in the U.S. Treasury. Although the land was ceded to the United States, nearly all the early treaties permitted the Indians to continue using the land for fishing and hunting. When one bears in mind that the means of subsistence were not taken from the Indian, and that the land in itself, or the timber on the land, meant little to the Indian—he was neither farmer nor lumberman—one can more readily understand how the chiefs and headmen of the bands could with justice affix their signatures to the treaties, in many instances, so unfair to their tribes.

ALLOTMENTS AND TAX EXEMPTIONS UNDER THE TREATIES
OF 1854 AND 1855

The system of allotments for the Chippewa began with the treaty made at La Pointe, Wisconsin, on September 30, 1854, a treaty between the

United States Government "and the Chippewa Indians of Lake Superior and the Mississippi by their chiefs and headmen."

Article 2 of the treaty provided for the patenting of eighty acres to each mixed blood over twenty-one years of age, while Article 3 made provision for the granting of eighty acres to other Indians as well. Article 3 reads as follows:

> The United States will define the boundaries of the reserved tracts, when-
> ever it may be necessary, by actual survey, and the President may, from
> time to time, at his discretion, cause the whole to be surveyed, and may
> assign to each head of a family or single person over twenty-one years of
> age, eighty acres of land for his or their separate use; and he may, at his
> discretion, as fast as the occupants become capable of transacting their
> own affairs, issue patents therefore to such occupants, with such restric-
> tions of the power of alienation as he may see fit to impose. And he may
> also at his discretion, make rules and regulations, respecting the disposi-
> tion of lands in case of the death of the head of a family, or single person
> occupying the same, or in case of its abandonment by them. And he may
> also assign other lands in exchange for mineral lands, if such be found in
> tracts herein set apart . . . [12]

A treaty between the United States and the Minnesota Chippewa in the following year, February 22, 1855, again authorized the President to assign "a reasonable quantity of land, in one body, not to exceed eighty acres in any case," to the head of each family, or single person over twenty-one years of age. It furthermore provided "said tracts to be exempt from taxation, levy, sale, or forfeiture; . . ."[13]

ESTABLISHING OF WHITE EARTH RESERVATION BY THE TREATY OF 1867

The treaty of March 19, 1867, is probably the most significant one of the treaties when it is studied in the light of social and economic problems of the White Earth Indians of today. The Chippewa bands of the Mississippi by it ceded lands estimated to contain about two million acres in return for which they were to receive a fair equivalent from the United States Government.

Article 2 of the treaty reads:

> In order to provide a suitable farming region for the said bands there is
> hereby set apart for their use a tract of land, to be located in a square form
> as nearly as possible, with lines corresponding to the Government sur-
> veys; which reservation shall include White Earth Lake and Rice Lake,
> and contain thirty-six townships of land: . . . [14]

Furthermore the Chippewa on the above tract of land were to be provided with the following: the erection and support of schools; the erec-

tion of a saw-mill with grist-mill attached; the erection of houses for such of the Indians as should remove to the reservation; cattle, horses, and farming utensils with the advice of the chiefs; a physician, and necessary medicines; and with "provisions, clothing, or such other articles as the President may determine, to be paid to them immediately on their removal to their new reservations."[15]

Undoubtedly in the eyes of the Government the above was considered a fair equivalent, but it appears most impracticable so far as the Chippewa were concerned. They were a people who had not yet advanced beyond the stage of hunting and food gathering. From a people who had roamed at will over millions of acres, they were now expected to confine themselves to an area containing less than half a million acres. From a roaming people of no formal education, living in wigwams or bark houses, grinding corn by hand with pestle and mortar and without domesticated animals, they were suddenly provided with means for formal education, for log or frame houses, for the grinding of corn and grain by means of machinery, for stock-raising and farming.

In retrospect, one wonders how anyone could have expected that a people, with a distinct, well-established, and well-integrated culture, should be ready to accept a manner of living so intrinsically different from theirs as is the European, for no other reason than that provisions for it were made in a treaty. Although the impact was unintentional, it has done something to the Chippewa; it has done something to them spiritually. From an independent and distinctive people, they have become one lacking initiative, incentive, enthusiasm, independence, self-respect.

The treaty, furthermore, provided for encouragement in agricultural pursuits. Any Indian man or woman, as soon as he had ten acres under cultivation, was to be given a certificate for forty acres, and an additional forty acres each time that he placed another ten under cultivation and so on, until a total of one hundred sixty acres had been certified to any one Indian. Such land was to be non-taxable and inalienable except to another member of the tribe.[16]

A final provision for adaptation to a new social order was made in Article 8 of the treaty:

> For the purpose of protecting and encouraging the Indians, parties to this treaty, in their efforts to become self-sustaining by means of agriculture, and the adoption of the habits of civilized life, it is hereby agreed that, in case of the commission by any of the said Indians of crimes against life or property, the person charged with such crimes may be arrested, upon the demand of the agent, by the sheriff of the county of Minnesota in which

said reservation may be located, and when so arrested may be tried, and if convicted, punished in the same manner as if he were not a member of an Indian tribe.[17]

GENERAL ALLOTMENT ACT OF 1887

The General Allotment Act was passed by Congress on February 8, 1887. By it, lands were to be allotted to any Indian according to the following:

To each head of a family, one-quarter of a section;
To each single person over eighteen years of age, one-eighth of a section;
To each orphan child under eighteen years of age, one-eighth of a section; and
To each other single person under eighteen years of age then living or to be born prior to the date of the order of the President directing an allotment of the lands embraced on any reservation, one-sixteenth of a section.

The Indians were permitted to select their own allotment, heads of families selecting for their minor children, and the United States agent for each orphan child.[18] Under this act many of the White Earth Indians took their allotments.

THE ACT OF JANUARY 14, 1889

"An act for the relief and civilization of the Chippewa Indians of the state of Minnesota," sometimes called the Nelson Act, was enacted on January 14, 1889.[19] It provided for a commission of three men to be appointed by the President who were to negotiate with all the bands of Chippewa in Minnesota for the cession of their remaining lands in the state, excepting the White Earth and the Red Lake reservations, and for as much of these two reservations as was not needed to provide allotments for the Minnesota Chippewa. The Red Lake Indians were to be allotted on the Red Lake Reservation; all others, on the White Earth. The act was to become effective on all reservations, except Red Lake, upon the consent in writing of two-thirds of all adult males over eighteen years of age in the band occupying the reservation. On the Red Lake Reservation it was to become effective upon the written consent of two-thirds of the male adults of all the Chippewa of Minnesota.

The ceded lands were to be surveyed and subdivided into forty-acre lots and classified as pine lands or as agricultural lands. The former were to be appraised and sold at public auction, notices being inserted once each week for four successive weeks in one newspaper of general circulation in Minneapolis, St. Paul, Duluth, and Crookston, Minnesota; Chicago, Illinois; Milwaukee, Wisconsin; Detroit, Michigan; Philadelphia and Williamsport, Pennsylvania; and Boston, Massachusetts. The agricultural lands were entered under the Homestead Law at a price of $1.25 per acre.

All money accruing from the disposal of lands, after deducting that needed for expenses connected with carrying out the provisions of the act, was to be deposited with the U.S. Treasury to the credit of all the Chippewa of Minnesota, drawing five per cent interest for fifty years following the date when the last allotments had been made. Three-fourths of the interest was to be distributed annually in per-capita payments, and one-fourth was "to be devoted exclusively to the establishment and maintenance of a system of free schools among said Indians, in their midst and for their benefit." At the end of the fifty years the original and permanent fund was to be distributed, in equal shares, to all Minnesota Chippewa then enrolled.

The act, furthermore, provided that no Chippewa in Minnesota was to be deprived of an allotment which had already been made to him without his consent. Any Indian, too, might, if he so wished, take his allotment on the reservation on which he was residing at the time of the act.

Various bands refused to leave their place of habitat and settlement and be removed to the White Earth Reservation, with the result that Chippewa of Minnesota today are found not only on the reservations of White Earth and Red Lake but also on those of Leech Lake, Nett Lake, Vermilion, Grand Portage, and Fond du Lac. One band, known today as the Non-removable Mille Lacs Band, living on other than Indian lands, by refusing to move from its place of settlement obliged the United States Government to purchase for it a habitat, namely the shores of Mille Lacs. (See Appendix B.)

To the fund, which has been accruing from the sale of timber permitted by the treaty, now known as the Chippewa of Minnesota Fund, have been added sums arising from the sale of town sites. Periodically, annuity and per-capita payments, drawn on the fund, are issued to the Indians on the roll. The most recent issues were a per-capita payment made in the spring of 1934 amounting to $25.00 per person, and an annuity payment of $3.00 per person, in 1937.

TIMBER AND ALLOTMENT SALES, 1904 AND 1906

By an act of Congress of 1904, all Chippewa of Minnesota were privileged to sell timber found on their allotments.[20] Lumber companies eagerly and readily bought the timber, Indians neither appreciating its value nor its use. With the sale of timber, boom days began for the White Earth Chippewa.

Two years later the Clapp Act, an act of Congress dated June 21, 1906, provided for the removal of all restrictions on the sale of allotments of land held by mixed-bloods on the White Earth Reservation.[21] The act, however, did not define a mixed-blood, nor was there an authentic legal roll designating the blood status of the Indians. Indians who knew of the provision of the act, and who were eager to sell their lands, vouched by affidavits that they were mixed-bloods, whereupon they were permitted to sell their lands. On the other hand, land buyers who were interested in purchasing certain allotments could usually do so without much difficulty by securing witnesses who swore affidavits that the Indian in question was of mixed-blood.

Allotment sales increased and Indians became wealthy, some of them receiving from $10,000 to $20,000. Storing the superfluous, or investing it, was not part of the economic heritage of the Chippewa. In fact, money was not part of their culture pattern, and since its value was not appreciated, their easily gotten wealth was soon spent. Before long, those who had sold their allotments were not only landless, but money-less.

The Clapp Act provided that twenty-five years after its passage all mixed-blood allotments became fee patents and therefore taxable. Allotments not sold often became tax delinquent and were taken over by the state. The older Indians tell how bewildered they were when the word "tax" was first introduced into their vocabulary. Its meaning seemed incomprehensible to them. The land which had been given to them by the President was now being taken from them for tax. Was "tax" a higher chief than the President, or who was he, inquired some? Other Indians lost their lands to money lenders in foreclosed mortgages. In 1934, only one in every twelve Chippewa on the White Earth Reservation owned his original allotment.[22] In 1938 probably fewer than four hundred Indians of a total population of eight thousand owned any land; most of them were squatters or renters.

RECENT LAND PURCHASES BY U.S. GOVERNMENT FOR
WHITE EARTH INDIANS

The United States Government has given thought within recent years of re-establishing the White Earth Indians on land. Forty homes were built on plots of land ranging from three to twenty acres each, partitioned out of lands formerly used as farm and garden sites for the U.S. Government Boarding School at White Earth. The homes were opened for occupancy in 1937 and by a plan of amortization were available for ownership to the Indians.

A land purchasing program for Indian occupancy on the White Earth Reservation was also under way. Funds available for such purchases were those of the U.S. resettlement program and of the Indian Reorganization Act. By means of these funds, approximately sixty thousand acres had been acquired for Indians on the White Earth Reservation.

U.S. BUREAU OF INDIAN AFFAIRS AND THE INDIAN
REORGANIZATION ACT, 1934

Previous to 1824, the policies of the United States Government relative to Indians were regulated by the occasion or by the problem to be solved. In 1824, however, a Bureau of Indian Affairs was established under the U.S. Department of War. It remained here until 1849 when by an act of Congress it was transferred to the Department of the Interior where it is located at the present time.

The most recent expression of the policies of the United States Government relative to the Indians is found in the Indian Reorganization Act, generally known as the Wheeler–Howard Act of June 18, 1934. It prohibits future allotments and the sale of Indian land except by tribes; it authorizes annual appropriation for purchases of land for landless Indians; it enables Indians voluntarily to return their individual holdings to the protection of tribal status; it authorizes a revolving loan and credit fund, the use of which is restricted to tribes that organize and incorporate so as to create community responsibility.[23]

The Chippewa under the jurisdiction of the Consolidated Chippewa Agency, namely those on the reservations of White Earth, Nett Lake, Leech Lake, Grand Portage, Fond du Lac, and Mille Lacs, had availed themselves of the privileges of the Reorganization Act, and organized under the corporate title of the Minnesota Chippewa Tribe. Their constitution received official approval of the Secretary of the Interior on July 24, 1936. The purpose and function of the organization as stated in the constitution is "to conserve and develop tribal resources and to promote the conservation and development of individual Indian trust property; to promote the general welfare of the members of the tribe; to preserve and maintain justice for its members and otherwise exercise all powers granted and provided the Indians and to take advantage of the privileges afforded by the Act of June 18, 1934 . . ."[24]

In order to function as a legal and a responsible body the tribe drew up the Corporate Charter of the Minnesota Chippewa Tribe and received its ratification on November 13, 1937. Its purpose of incorporation as expressed in the charter is "to further the economic development of the Minnesota Chippewa Tribe by conferring upon the said Tribe certain corporate rights, powers, privileges and immunities; to secure for the members of the Tribe an assured economic independence; and to provide for the proper exercise by the Tribe of various functions heretofore performed by the Department of the Interior, . . ."[25]

INDIANS AND THE STATE OF MINNESOTA

As may be recalled, the Federal Government, as early as 1867, shared with Minnesota its responsibility relative to law and order. By the treaty of 1867, any Chippewa committing a crime might be arrested by the sheriff of the county in which the reservation was located, conveyed to trial, and if convicted, punished according to law.[26]

Furthermore, by a Congressional act of June, 1924, all Indians became citizens of the United States and therefore subject to all laws of the states in which they reside, excepting that no state may encroach upon the title to property held by the United States Government for Indian occupancy, nor upon the jurisdiction which the Federal Government exercises over certain offenses when committed by an Indian upon a reservation; nor may a state impair the protection of the interests of Indians by the Federal Government.[27]

The Johnson–O'Malley Act of April 16, 1934, authorized the U.S. Office of Indian Affairs to make contracts with the various states for services to Indians in the fields of education, health, and social service.[28]

Both the Minnesota State Department of Education and the Minnesota State Department of Health have made definite efforts to cooperate with the Federal Government by rendering service to the Indians of the state. The former has, by special arrangement, disbursed an annual federal appropriation of $100,000 to public schools in which Minnesota Indians are being educated. The latter maintains the Chippewa Health Unit at Cass Lake, Minnesota.

SOURCES

1. Clark Wissler, *The American Indian, An Introduction to the Anthropology of the New World* (New York: Oxford University Press, American Branch, 1922), p. 403–404.
2. Alanson Skinner, *Notes on the Eastern Cree and Northern Saulteaux* (Anthropological Papers of the American Museum of Natural History, IX, 1 [1911]), p. 117.
   Frances Densmore, *Chippewa Customs* (U.S. Bureau of American Ethnology Bulletin 86 [1929]), p. 75.
   Frederick Webb Hodge, *Handbook of American Indians North of Mexico* (U.S. Bureau of American Ethnology Bulletin 30, Part 1 [1907]), p. 277.
3. William Warren, *History of the Ojibways* (in Collections of the Minnesota Historical Society, V [1885]), p. 76, 79.
4. *Op. cit.,* p. 117.
5. *Op. cit.,* p. 277.
6. Louise Phelps Kellogg, (ed.) *Early Narratives of the Northwest, 1634–1699* (New York: Charles Scribner's Sons, 1917), p. 23, 135.
7. Hodge, *op. cit.,* p. 278.
8. *Ibid.*
9. George Copway, *The Traditional History and Characteristic Sketches of the Ojibway Nation* (Boston: Benj. B. Mussey & Co., 1851), p. 170.
10. Hodge, *op, cit.,* p. 280.
11. Charles J. Kappler, (ed.) *Indian Affairs: Laws and Treaties* (Washington: Government Printing Office, 1903), II, 13–754 *passim.*
12. *Ibid.,* II, 486.
13. *Ibid.,* II, 514.
14. *Ibid.,* II, 753.
15. *Ibid.*
16. *Ibid.,* II, 754.
17. *Ibid.*
18. Jay P. Kinney, *A Continent Lost–A Civilization Won, Indian Land Tenure in America* (Baltimore: Johns Hopkins Press, 1937), p. 199.
19. Charles J. Kappler, (ed.) *Indian Affairs: Laws and Treaties* (Washington: Government Printing Office, 1903), I, 302–306 *passim.*
20. Charles J. Kappler, (ed.) *Indian Affairs: Laws and Treaties* (Washington: Government Printing Office, 1913), III, 55.
21. *Ibid.,* III, 220.

22. *Report of January 19, 1935 of the Commissioner of the U.S. Bureau of Indian Affairs to the U.S. Secretary of the Interior* (Manuscript).

23. Kinney, *op. cit.*, p. 310–320.

24. *Constitution and By-laws of the Minnesota Chippewa Tribe* (Washington: Government Printing Office, 1936), p. 1.

25. *Corporate Charter of the Minnesota Chippewa Tribe of the Consolidated Chippewa Agency* (Washington: Government Printing Office, 1938), p. 1.

26. Kappler, *op. cit.*, II, 754.

27. *Ibid.*, IV, 420.

28. *U.S. Statutes at Large*, Vol. 48, Ch. 147.

CHAPTER I

Physical Setting and Population Basis of the White Earth Reservation

LOCATION AND RESOURCES

The White Earth Reservation comprises thirty-two townships, or approximately seven hundred fifty thousand acres. Four of the townships, Nos. 143, 144, 145, 146, N., Range 38, W., lie in the southwest corner of Clearwater County; twelve, Nos. 141, 142, N., Ranges 37, 38, 39, 40, 41, 42, W., are found in Becker County; the remaining sixteen form Mahnomen County, which county, therefore, lies wholly in the reservation. The reservation is thirty-six miles from north to south and thirty miles from east to west except for a portion in Becker County which is thirty-six miles east and west. (See Appendix B.)

The topography of the reservation shows rather distinct rolling hills, typical upland prairie lands, level marshy valleys, and beautiful lakes and creeks. Rolling land of a rich loam is found north and west of a line drawn from southwest to northeast corners. This land is partly covered with deciduous trees of non-marketable value, and tapers off rather sharply to level prairie lands on the border. Much of this area is now in farms owned by whites. The land to the south and east of the southwest-northeast line is sandy soil and is strictly cut-over land with struggling coniferous and aspen growths. The soil is unsuited for agriculture but could be used for pasturage. This section at the time of allotments was covered with virgin pine of white and Norway types.

The maximum elevation of the area is 1365 feet. The average rainfall approximates twenty-three inches. The growing season is approximately 113 days extending from May 28 to September 17.

TRANSPORTATION AND COMMUNICATION

The "Soo" line, the only railroad transportation crossing the reservation, is about six miles from the west boundary of the reservation and runs

nearly parallel to it. It connects with the main line of the Northern
Pacific at Detroit Lakes, Minnesota, ten miles from the southern boundary of the reservation, and at Erskine, just north of the northern boundary, with a branch line of the Great Northern running into Duluth. A
good system of gravel roads connects all parts of the reservation and
joins with state highway No. 59 which crosses the reservation from
north to south, running nearly parallel to the "Soo" Railroad. State highway No. 59 connects with U.S. No. 10 at Detroit Lakes and with U.S.
No. 2 at Erskine.

Communication by telephone is poor. A message from White Earth
to Ponsford, only twenty-nine miles away must be sent by way of
Minneapolis some two hundred miles from either village.

MARKET CENTERS

The principal market centers on the reservation are the towns located on
the "Soo" line, namely Bijou, Mahnomen, Waubun, Ogema, and
Callaway. The nearest markets off the reservation are Detroit Lakes (3500
pop.) about ten miles from the southwest corner of the reservation; Park
Rapids (2500 pop.) about eighteen miles from the southeast corner; and
Bagley (850 pop.) about twelve miles from the northeast corner.

POPULATION COMPOSITION AND BLOOD QUANTUM

The Indian population of the reservation and the supposedly correct
quantum of Indian blood of each member is recorded in the tribal roll at
the Consolidated Chippewa Agency. An Indian may be on the roll
because of his birth and residence on the reservation, or because of his
tribal inheritance rights, he himself residing anywhere in the United
States or in a foreign country.

Mixture of blood in the bands now composing the White Earth
Indians began with the arrival of the French voyageurs in the eighteenth
century. Voyageurs were followed by loggers and lumbermen of various
nations who readily intermarried with Indian women. Many of these
white men, fathers of mixed-bloods, desirous that their children be given
opportunities and benefits, were in no small degree responsible for the
favors bestowed upon mixed-bloods in treaties and Congressional acts.
Full-bloods, anxious to share the supposedly better lot of their mixed-
blood brethren, were quite willing, when the opportunity presented
itself, to have papers drawn up and affidavits filed that they, too, were
mixed-bloods. As may be recalled, this was the case at the time of the
sale of timber and allotments in 1906 with the result that there were

many fraudulent sales. No authentic roll giving the blood status of the White Earth Indians was in existence in 1906.

Due largely to the influence of persons imbued with a sense of justice, a commission was sent to the White Earth Reservation by the U.S. Bureau of Indian Affairs to investigate these fraudulent land sales. One of the results of the investigation was the establishing of an official roll, commonly known as the Hinton Roll of 1910. Many Indians and whites alike are convinced that the blood quantum recorded in the Hinton Roll is not accurate. Word was circulated among the Indians shortly after the arrival of the commission that the latter was empowered to return lands to full-bloods. Many mixed-bloods, anxious to have the advantages of full-bloods, gave full-blood as their quantum. Indians say that the Hinton Roll, therefore, has two sets of fraudulent blood quanta in its list, namely full-bloods who in 1906 declared themselves mixed-bloods and mixed-bloods who in 1910 declared themselves full-bloods. The result of this confusion is that no accurate information is now available as to blood quantum of the White Earth Indians. Indians themselves when discussing blood quantum noted that in all probability the degree of Indian blood is higher than one might expect.

The White Earth Indians, as well as other Chippewa, are aware that their rolls need purging, and have therefore provided for a revision in the constitution for the Minnesota Chippewa Tribe. The governing body of the tribe may make corrections in the rolls subject to the approval of the Secretary of the Interior.

Assimilation is slowly progressing. Whites of various nationalities are married to persons of Indian descent on the White Earth Reservation, several of them being members of the one hundred fifty families of this study.

ENROLLED WHITE EARTH INDIANS

According to the annual statistical report of the Consolidated Chippewa Agency to the U.S. Office of Indian Affairs of January 1, 1938, the total Indian population on the White Earth Reservation roll was 8429. This number was more than fifty per cent of the population of the entire consolidated jurisdiction which covered six reservations. Of the 8429 persons, 5805 or sixty-eight per cent resided on the White Earth Reservation; 308, on other reservations; and 2316, in white communities. In the total number, females exceeded males by sixty-one. Only two-thirds of one per cent of the total population of the state of Minnesota is Indian.

The exact number of families residing on the reservation was not known. The social and economic survey of 1934 reported fourteen hundred fifty; the figures of the assistant to the superintendent for the Consolidated Chippewa Agency approximated eleven hundred. The figures dealing with the average size of the families, however, are in greater agreement. The social and economic survey reported 5.28 number of persons per family, as the average. The Chippewa Health Unit, basing its estimate on a fair sample, reported 5.14; the findings of this study based on one hundred fifty families is 5.65.

Vital statistics for the White Earth Reservation for the year 1937 reported two hundred three births and ninety-seven deaths.

COMMUNITIES ON THE WHITE EARTH RESERVATION

Living in groups of families, somewhat scattered over an area but within easy reach of other members of the group, is traditional among the Chippewa. Ties which bound families together into groups were usually those of blood, although mere friendship with one or the other family of the group might give membership in it. Occasions for permanent winter habitat for a group were some natural resource, such as good hunting grounds or a spring. Favorite spots were sugar bushes on the shores of lakes since the nearness of maple trees did not necessitate moving camp in the early spring when the sap began to flow. During the spring, summer, and fall, several families of the group moved about together, following seasonal occupations, such as maple-sugar making, berry picking, or wild-rice gathering. Group life of this type still existed in parts of the White Earth Reservation when this study was made, activities conforming in large part to the traditional pattern. One heard people speak of the Le Duc community, the Island Lake group, the Brunette families, etc.

Village life, however, as we know it today, was not known to the early Chippewa. At times, it is true, all the members of the band met to confer among themselves regarding peace or war, or for the celebration of the Midē wiwin, and although such gatherings presented the appearance of a village, there was no permanency about them. Today, however, a fair number of the Indians on the White Earth Reservation live in villages. Villages grew up around U.S. agency headquarters primarily. Mixed bloods, in whose rearing Chippewa and European cultures had fairly well amalgamated, found living near white people to their liking, as well as to their advantage. Sales of allotments and timber gave them sufficient money to build homes of some respectable size and appearance. Small numbers of full-bloods, too, moved into the villages, usually however, remaining on the outskirts. Some old Indians gave as the reason for their removal into the village the need of being nearer the source of supplies. Their old sources, those of hunting and fishing, were no longer available to them; the new ones, those supplying annuities and per-capita payments, were found in the agency.

The White Earth Reservation in 1938 presented three types of groups or communities, each having distinguishing characteristics. Along the state highway and the "Soo" line were found the incorporated towns or villages of Callaway, Ogema, Waubun, Mahnomen, and Bijou. In these towns, except in parts of Mahnomen, it was difficult to select the Indians from among the whites. Another type of group was found farther inland in the un-incorporated villages of White Earth, Ponsford, Naytahwaush, and Beaulieu. The larger group in these villages considered itself Indian, and was so classified by others. A third group was found in the communities of scattered families in various parts of the reservation. These maintained some identity and unity, and one heard them spoken of as the communities of Maple Grove, Elbow Lake, Round Lake, Rice Lake, Pine Bend, and Island Lake.

The towns along the state highway presented the appearance of middle-western towns and differed in no respect from them. Each had a main street flanked by grocery stores, dry-goods stores, a bank or two, a drug store or two, a post office—usually located in one of the stores—and several liquor shops. On side streets were found churches, schools, and places of residence, ranging from fine structures of brick, with well-kept yards, to damaged, unpainted frame buildings in which the poor lived. Mahnomen differed from the above in that on its outskirts was found a settlement of tar-paper shacks and one-room frame houses in which not only Indians but also whites lived. Among the Mahnomen folk this settlement was known as "Copper Town."

The remaining communities on the reservation, however, had distinctive features. They were so characterized both by the Indians themselves and by the whites on the reservation who dealt with them. Work among them left little doubt as to the validity of these characterizations.

White Earth, the largest of the villages, comprised about 169 families. It presented the appearance of a village of unpainted, inartistic, in many cases, damaged, frame buildings—buildings whose history dated back to the boom days of the sale of allotments and of timber rights. Forty rehabilitation houses, erected by the U.S. Office of Indian Affairs, extended along streets to the north and west and over an area east of the village. These houses were of varying design and presented an appearance of neatness. The community of White Earth was decidedly lacking in an orderly social system, in a sense of community responsibility, in co-operative constructive action for social betterment. The village had the reputation amongst its own better class, as well as amongst the people on the reservation and in the surrounding area, of being a place of drunken debaucheries and loose moral conduct. It appeared as though social controls of the old Chippewa culture had gone out of the community and none had replaced them. It was difficult to think of White Earth village as a community of Indians; it was pathetic to think of it as one of whites! People in it resented the yoke of Governmental paternalism. They complained that although they had drawn up a constitution and bylaws which was to give the Chippewa rights over tribal matters, the will of the Secretary of the Interior was the deciding factor.

Ponsford, consisting of approximately 114 families, gave the impression of a town of tar-paper dwellings. Old Chippewa customs still existed in the community, among them the Grand Medicine Dance. The group had a larger per cent of near full-bloods than any other on the reservation and a feeling of Indians-versus-whites existed. Its people gave the impression as being rather serene and contented. They thought conditions better than before W.P.A., and they were not much worried about the future. Its reputation was that it was somewhat better morally than White Earth village. Drinking was its greatest evil, but the inhabitants of the village were not greatly disturbed over this for "beer-joints will move out as soon as W.P.A. ends!" They had heard that the President could not give W.P.A. jobs much longer, for the country was going bankrupt.

Naytahwaush, a community including approximately ninety-two families, consisted of homes of tar-paper shacks, frame houses, and log cabins. The interior of homes ranged from indescribably filthy ones to some of the best homes on the reservation. The people appeared to be of a peaceful type. They were friendly and seemed busy about their own affairs. Many were worried about social conditions in the community, the result of the sale of liquor, and had fears that "soon things would be as bad as in White Earth." Morals were none too high.

Beaulieu, the fourth largest community off the highway, consisted of approximately fifteen families. Its frame houses and tar-paper shacks were nestled in a grove of trees. A fine spirit of neighborliness existed among them and a most cordial welcome was extended to visitors. They were a pleasant people and felt that they were being well treated by every one.

Elbow Lake community consisted of about twenty-five families located on the beautiful shores of Elbow Lake. Many families lived in four-room, government-owned houses, rent being free. They impressed one as rather saddened or discouraged, and as lacking ambition.

The Maple Grove community, some twelve families, were scattered through an area from the south of Lake McCraney to White Earth Lake. They preferred living scattered and apart from other families. "We live near enough to other people to visit them and not to feel alone; but best of all we can keep our children home and know what they are doing!" They were an exceedingly friendly group.

The Round Lake community, a total of twelve families, lived scattered in groups of three or four families. They traded at Ponsford, but did not admire social conditions there. In fact, they resented a Ponsford family that had moved into the community and "hoped to force them back to their village, by freezing them out!"

The Rice Lake, the Pine Bend, and the Island Lake communities, each consisting of no more than twelve families, lay scattered along the edges of lakes in the northeast quarter of the reservation. They were a contented group, little tainted by the vices of European civilization. They loved their isolated life and were convinced that nature about them offered ample recompenses. There was an independence evident among them that was quite unique on the reservation.

SOURCES

A. LITERATURE CITED

E. J. Carlson, *Annual Forestry and Grazing Report for Fiscal Year of 1937* (Duluth: Consolidated Chippewa Agency). (Manuscript).

1937 Census of the White Earth Reservation. 1938 Supplemental Census and Addition Roll. 1938 Deduction Roll (Duluth: Consolidated Chippewa Agency). (Manuscript).

Land records (Duluth: Consolidated Chippewa Agency). (Manuscript).

Lists Showing the Degree of Indian Blood of Certain Persons Holding Land upon the White Earth Reservation in Minnesota and a List Showing the Date of Death of Certain Persons Who Held Land upon Such Reservation (Washington: Government Printing Office, 1911). (Commonly called *Hinton Roll*).

Shirley McKinsey, *Report of 1937–1938 Based on a Survey of the Six Chippewa Reservations under the Consolidated Chippewa Agency* (Duluth: Consolidated Chippewa Agency). (Manuscript).

Survey of Conditions of the Indians in the United States: Hearings of 1933 before a Subcommittee of the Committee on Indian Affairs, United States Senate, Seventy-third Congress (Washington: Government Printing Office, 1934).

Tribal Roll of the Minnesota Chippewa Indians (Duluth: Consolidated Chippewa Agency, 1938). (Manuscript).

B. PERSONS INTERVIEWED

Louis Balsam, Ph.D., field representative to the Commissioner of Indian Affairs, and superintendent of the Consolidated Chippewa Agency, Duluth, Minnesota.

Chippewa Indian men and women of the White Earth Reservation.

Melvin Hunt, assistant to the superintendent of the Consolidated Chippewa Agency, White Earth Reservation.

James Munnell, land clerk, Consolidated Chippewa Agency, Duluth, Minnesota.

Elizabeth Rowlette, clerk, division of statistics, Consolidated Chippewa Agency, Duluth, Minnesota.

CHAPTER II

Opportunities for Complete Living on the White Earth Reservation in 1938

ECONOMIC OPPORTUNITIES AND FACTORS

Cash income for most of the White Earth Reservation families for the years 1934–1938 came from employment on projects of the U.S. Works Progress Administration (W.P.A.), National Youth Administration (N.Y.A.), and from two divisions of the Consolidated Chippewa Agency, namely the Division of Roads and the Indian Division of the Civilian Conservation Corps (C.C.C.–I.D.). Several persons were either earning their living, or increasing their income, by private efforts.

W.P.A. projects for both men and women were located at White Earth and at Ponsford. Incomes from them amounted to $44.00 a month, being paid in bi-weekly checks of $22.00 each.

Headquarters of the C.C.C.–I.D. for the employment of men of the White Earth Reservation only was located at Naytahwaush. Monthly incomes for unskilled laborers working under its direction amounted to $45.00; persons of trade or other abilities were receiving as much as $130.00 a month. A camp under this same division, to which men from all reservations of the Consolidated Chippewa Jurisdiction were admitted, was located on the Nett Lake Reservation. Income from employment in it amounted to $30.00 a month.

N.Y.A. employment was assigned by the counties, and young men and women so employed were found in various parts of the reservation, receiving an income of $12.00 a month.

The Division of Roads of the Indian Service employed both skilled and unskilled labor, wages ranging from $45.00 to $150.00 a month.

Employment for men under the various projects consisted of the building of roads and truck trails, of fire prevention and suppression, of the building of dams for water control, of wild-rice culture and development, of re-forestation, of the building of foot and vehicle bridges, and

21

of the wrecking of abandoned government buildings using the salvage for the building of a district school. Women employed by W.P.A. were engaged in sewing projects sponsored by the counties.

In pre-depression days the lumbering industry offered work to some Indians. More recently, however, the only employment in this industry for White Earth Indians, and very few were so employed, was that of preparing pulpwood for markets in Duluth and Superior. Firewood was also being cut for profit, markets being found in the treeless plains areas immediately to the west of the reservation.

A small number of Indians were engaged in raising grain and live-stock. The annual extension report for 1937 to the U.S. Bureau of Indian Affairs stated that two hundred of the White Earth Reservation Indians were farming and that eight were specializing in raising stock. Stock rais-ing might well be encouraged, since much of the land in the area could be used for pasturage. Excellent opportunities, too, for marketing cream were offered by co-operative creameries located at several points along the "Soo" line. A few Indians were owners of poultry, cattle, sheep, goats, swine, or horses, and derived some income from these.

During harvesting season some Indians hired out in the grain fields of the Red River valley and in the potato farms near Ogema. Most of the families increased their income by kitchen gardens, eighty of those living in Becker County having entered the county garden contest.

Native crafts which ought to be a source of income for many of the women and which, incidentally, could profitably and pleasantly occupy their leisure time, is fast dying out. Marketing opportunities were offered by the Detroit Lakes Chamber of Commerce and by the Chippewa Indian Co-operative Association located at Cass Lake about one hun-dred miles from the White Earth Reservation. Any Indian selling to the latter automatically becomes a member, shares in the dividends, and has a vote in the election of its board of directors. It extends its marketing to beadwork, birch-bark work, bows and arrows, woven rugs, bulrush mats, wild rice, maple sugar, fresh berries and fuel wood.

For most of the Chippewa on the White Earth Reservation opportu-nities for living on any but a subsistence standard were non-existent. Persons in the U.S. Indian Service on the reservation estimated that the average yearly income per family was $577.00.

GOVERNMENTAL FACTORS AND FACILITIES

As citizens of the United States by act of Congress of June 2, 1924, all Indians may vote in primary, general, and special elections. The percentage of Indians on the White Earth Reservation who availed themselves of this privilege was not ascertainable since Indian votes were indistinguishable from those cast by whites in the same locality. If one may base an estimate, however, on the sample of one hundred fifty families covered in this study, approximately sixty-nine per cent voted.

In addition to having the franchise as citizens of the United States, each Chippewa man and woman on the tribal roll who has reached the age of twenty-one has the right to cast a vote in the selection of the tribal delegate who is to represent his community in the general tribal council of the Minnesota Chippewa Tribe. This right is granted by the constitution and by-laws of the Minnesota Chippewa Tribe. The Minnesota Chippewa, furthermore, have rights in their own local self-government, for Article XI of the constitution stipulates that "Each reservation and district or community may govern itself in local matters in accordance with its custom and may obtain, if it so desires, from the tribal executive committee a charter setting forth its organization and powers." The formation of local councils as permitted by the constitution was being discussed by the White Earth Indians in the summer of 1938. Most of the communities, however, had local councils composed of every man, woman, and child in the community, which were claimed to be a continuation of the traditional councils of their tribal bands. Traditionally these were largely advisory bodies for chiefs and headsmen in local matters or at general tribal meetings. Today they are mere minority groups and appear to do little constructive work for their own people. Their activities impress one as being those of vigilantes.

OPPORTUNITIES FOR RELIGIOUS EXPRESSION

The White Earth Reservation Indians hold membership in the traditional Chippewa religion, the Midē wiwin, and in the Catholic, the Episcopal, the Methodist, and the Gospel Alliance churches.

Members of the Midē wiwin meet and celebrate their ceremonial each spring and fall at Ponsford and at Elbow Lake, and at these times new members are admitted. Two preschool children were granted admission at Ponsford in June, 1938.

Catholic church buildings with resident priests are located in the towns of Callaway, Ogema, Waubun, and Mahnomen, and in the villages of White Earth, Ponsford, and Beaulieu. Masses are also said in mission churches at Naytahwaush, Round Lake, Island Lake, and in a schoolroom at Elbow Lake.

Episcopal churches with resident ministers are located in the villages of White Earth, Ponsford, and Naytahwaush.

A Methodist church with resident minister is found at Pine Bend. Gospel Alliance churches with resident ministers are located in the villages of White Earth and Naytahwaush.

HEALTH FACILITIES

The Indians on the White Earth Reservation have the advantage of both federal and state medical service. The U.S. Indian Service maintains a twenty-bed hospital in White Earth village. It is staffed by a full-time physician and three registered nurses. The hospital is equipped to give general medical care, to do X-ray photography, major and minor surgeries, and obstetrics. All cases on the reservation that needed hospitalization were sent to White Earth Hospital. Any patients, however, who needed attention which the hospital was not equipped to give, were transferred to the Detroit Lakes Hospital or to the University of Minnesota Hospital in Minneapolis. Crippled children received treatment at the Gillette State Hospital for Crippled Children in St. Paul.

Two physicians—with field nurses co-operating—conducted weekly clinics at Naytahwaush, Ponsford, Elbow Lake, Pine Bend, Beaulieu, and Mahnomen.

Field nurses were located at Naytahwaush and at Ponsford. The Naytahwaush nurse was responsible to the Minnesota State Health Unit No. 1 with headquarters at Bemidji, and rendered service exclusively to Indians on the White Earth Reservation. Her territory, however, did not cover Becker County. The latter group was served by the Ponsford nurse who was appointed by the U.S. Indian Service and was directly responsible to the sub-agency at White Earth.

The Chippewa Health Unit located at Cass Lake and maintained by the Minnesota State Department of Public Health was largely interested in public health matters, such as sanitation, the spread and control of communicable diseases, etc.

The U.S. Indian Service has constructed a wing at the Minnesota State Tuberculosis Sanitorium at Walker, Minnesota, and remunerates the state per day for services rendered Indian patients. The greatest mortality among the Chippewa was due to tuberculosis. The Minnesota State Department of Health Report for 1935 noted deaths due to tuberculosis as 458.3 per 100,000 for the Chippewa, while that for the Minnesota population in general was only 35.8.

During the summer of 1938, a health camp for underprivileged Chippewa children between the ages of six to twelve was conducted just north of Grand Marais, Minnesota. Fifty White Earth Reservation children were enrolled.

EDUCATION

The education division of the Minnesota Works Progress Administration has maintained a nursery school in the village of White Earth since 1935. The staff in 1938 consisted of a supervisor, three teachers, a cook, and three N.Y.A. girls, all but the supervisor and two of the teachers being Indians. Thirty-four children, ranging from two to six years of age, attended sixty hours of every two weeks. The program, like that of any nursery school, provided for physical examinations, corrective and preventive health treatment, for diet, for learning, and for rest. Objectives of the school centered largely about two activities: health for children and education for parents. Parent education was carried on by means of a mothers' and fathers' club.

All schools on the reservation, excepting St. Benedict's Mission School for Girls, were operated by the state of Minnesota, Indian and white children attending the same schools and having equal opportunities. Where walking distances were too great, school buses collected children, and children who could not be easily reached by buses were placed in boarding schools.

Boarding schools, admitting grade children, were St. Benedict's Mission School for Girls at White Earth, St. Mary's School for Boys and Girls at Red Lake, Minnesota, and the United States Government-operated schools at Pipestone in Minnesota, Wahpeton in North Dakota, Flandreau in South Dakota, and Haskell in Kansas.

High school education was offered in the local high schools at Waubun, Mahnomen, Detroit Lakes, and Park Rapids. A number of boys and girls attended these schools utilizing bus service. Boarding high schools were maintained by the United States Government at Flandreau and Haskell, the latter also offering two years of business training following the four years of high school.

Young men and women who desired to attend vocational schools or schools of higher learning could make loans from the division of education of the U.S. Indian Service.

Extension education in operation in 1937 and 1938 was being directed through a unit of the agricultural extension division of the Consolidated Chippewa Agency maintained at Naytahwaush. Among the activities were fourteen 4-H clubs, eight of which were led by Indian leaders. The work of the clubs was directly co-ordinated with that of the counties and followed the state program excepting in handicrafts projects.

Adult education was not well developed. Its scope in 1938 consisted of a series of lectures on poultry given by the extension field worker to the occupants of the rehabilitation houses at White Earth, to the activities of the fathers' and mothers' club of the nursery school, and to the activities of five homemakers' clubs.

Homemakers' clubs were probably contributing much to adult education so far as the mothers were concerned. Members of the various clubs–all clubs were led by Indian women–mapped out their own programs, with the assistance of the extension field worker. Programs usually centered around seasonal interests. One of the clubs adhered to the following program: Clothing, coats and caps were designed and sewed during the winter months; gardening and poultry-raising were discussed in the spring; methods of canning were taught in the summer; and quilts were made in the fall. Funds were raised in various ways. One club raised its funds by requiring dues of twenty-five cents per person per year, by fines of one cent assessed against all absentees or late comers, and by social functions in which the entire community participated. Purchases for the club, such as bolts of cloth, seeds, or Mason jars, were bought at wholesale or quantity prices. All work was voluntary, members duplicating their products whenever possible, taking one home and leaving the other for sale by the club.

Reading facilities on the reservation were practically nil. There was no circulating library. The only public library on the reservation was located at Mahnomen in the northwest corner of the reservation and was therefore not easily accessible to a large number. The high schools at Waubun and Mahnomen circulated books among their students, but only during the school year.

Local weekly newspapers, the Mahnomen *Pioneer,* the Detroit Lakes *News Tribune,* and the Detroit Lakes *Record,* had a number of subscribers among the Indians. Some, too, subscribed to the Sunday editions of the Minneapolis *Tribune,* the Minneapolis *Journal,* the St. Paul *Pioneer Press,* the St. Paul *Dispatch,* the Chicago *Tribune,* the Philadelphia *Enquirer,* the New York *Daily News,* and *Grit.* Many more purchased newspapers at general merchandise stores in their localities, or bought them from "peddlers" who brought them to their doors on Sunday.

Periodicals could be bought in some of the stores. Inquiries revealed that the ones generally purchased were *True Stories, True Confessions, True Romances, True Experiences,* and *True Detective.*

SOCIAL LIFE AND PROBLEMS

Wholesome recreational life on the reservation was practically non-existent. Of the traditional type of recreation which consisted largely of competitive games in which many of the community participated and the rest enjoyed non-participation none existed. Of the newer types, baseball and horse-shoe-throwing seemed to be the two most enjoyed.

Trained recreational leadership was entirely wanting. W.P.A. recreational projects, such as kitten ball, a community band, etc., were announced in the early summer of 1938 but only a few persons responded and these soon dropped out. Leaders claimed that it was difficult to get concerted action on anything among the young people.

In nearly all communities drinking to excess, accompanied by carousing and immoral conduct, formed the only group recreation. The villages of White Earth, Ponsford, Naytahwaush, and Ogema were known on the reservation as well as in the surrounding areas and communities as places where every pay-day brought its days and nights of moral degradation for a group of the people. The maintenance of law and order fell under the jurisdiction of the state, the counties, the townships, and the incorporated villages. It was quite evident that this responsibility did not weigh heavily on any of them.

Consumption of liquor was undoubtedly the greatest evil on the reservation. It was illegal to sell liquor to an Indian, and yet whites in every community sold liquor to persons who were easily distinguishable as Indians. In the days of prohibition not only was boot-legging carried on among the Indians, but Indians learnt the making of home-brew. White persons, in a position to know, as well as respectable Indians on the reservation, say that if the law forbidding the sale of liquor to the Indians were enforced, conditions would become as in prohibition days and that these were far more debasing than are those of the present time.

It was estimated, furthermore, that eighty-five per cent of all boys and girls between ten and eighteen years of age in White Earth village drank intoxicating liquor. Minors were frequently seen among adults in beer parlors and saloons in Ogema, and at a "joint" about one and one-half miles north of the village. Cases had been reported where clothing and food, given by counties as relief, were traded in, and accepted, for liquor.

Conditions at Ponsford, too, needed attention, for the following notice was posted there by the community worker: "To all N.Y.A. Employees in Pine Point Area: It has come to my attention that youths and girls who are employed in N.Y.A. projects here are frequenting the beer parlors and wasting their time and funds there. The purpose of those projects is to give employees funds to help in their support at home. It is not given to provide means for loitering around in beer parlors. Hereafter, when it is found that employees are habitual frequenters of beer parlors, it will be recommended that they be terminated from the various projects."

The annual statistical report of the Consolidated Chippewa Agency for the year 1937 shows the three counties in which White Earth Reservation is located to have made twenty-nine arrests of White Earth Reservation Indians during that year. Twenty of these were followed by convictions with penalties of ten days imprisonment in each case.

The only group of Indians on the reservation that had an adequate community center was Ponsford, the school auditorium lending itself well for this purpose. The village of White Earth is expected to have a center as soon as the auditorium of the new district school building is completed.

Moving pictures were shown in the towns along the state highway, as well as in White Earth and in Ponsford. Rather careful selections were being made in the last two places. Patrons enjoyed western and musical movies best.

SOCIAL TREATMENT

Indians of Minnesota, being citizens of the state, are committed to county or state institutions for remedial or preventive care, or for penal and correctional purposes.

The most recent figures available on the physically and mentally handicapped White Earth Indians were those of the social and economic survey of 1934. The survey enumerated a total of two hundred forty cases, namely forty-three as blind, fifty-six as crippled, forty-six as tubercular, thirty-two as invalids, seventy as aged, and three as mental.

Indigent aged and blind persons were cared for by the counties in which they resided from funds of the Social Security Act. On December 31, 1937, one hundred twenty-four White Earth Indians were receiving old age assistance from Becker County, eighty-three from Mahnomen County, and nineteen from Clearwater County. Four were receiving aid for the blind in Becker County, none in Clearwater County, and one in Mahnomen County, many of the blind, however, receiving old age assistance. Forty-four in Becker County were receiving aid for dependent children, none in Clearwater County, and two in Mahnomen.

Dependent children from broken homes, or from homes entirely inadequate economically or morally, were being cared for in either a U.S. Government boarding school or in one of the mission schools in either White Earth or Red Lake.

SOURCES

A. LITERATURE CITED

Annual Extension Report for Consolidated Chippewa Agency for 1937 (Duluth: Consolidated Chippewa Agency). (Manuscript).

Constitution and By-laws of the Minnesota Chippewa (Washington: Government Printing Office, 1936).

Corporate Charter of the Minnesota Chippewa Tribe of the Consolidated Chippewa Agency (Washington: Government Printing Office, 1938).

Indian Emergency Conservation Program, April 1, 1937 to June 30, 1938 (Duluth: Consolidated Chippewa Agency). (Manuscript).

Social and Economic Survey of the Consolidated Chippewa Agency of 1934 (Washington: U.S. Bureau of Indian Affairs). (Manuscript).

State of Minnesota Aid to Dependent Children Act, Adopted by the Legislature of 1937 (St. Paul: State Board of Control, 1937).

State of Minnesota Old Age Assistance Act, Adopted by Special Session of the Legislature of 1935–1936, Amended by Regular Session of the Legislature of 1937, and Including Other Laws Pertaining to Old Age Assistance Passed by 1937 Special Session of the Legislature (St. Paul: State Board of Control, 1937).

B. PERSONS INTERVIEWED

Louis Balsam, Ph.D., field representative to the Commissioner of Indian Affairs, and superintendent of the Consolidated Chippewa Agency, Duluth, Minnesota.

A. C. Beaulieu, former secretary of the tribal executive committee, Minnesota Chippewa Tribe, White Earth, Minnesota.

Lawrence De Haan, U.S. extension field worker, White Earth Reservation.

A. O. Hoghaug, secretary, Becker County welfare board, Detroit Lakes, Minnesota.

Melvin Hunt, assistant to the superintendent of the Consolidated Chippewa Agency, White Earth Reservation.

Helen Leach, social worker, Becker County, Detroit Lakes, Minnesota.

W. T. Lehnherr, community worker, White Earth Reservation.

Justine Leutmer, O.S.B., director, St. Benedict's Mission, White Earth Reservation.

Mary Long, clerk, individual Indian money, Consolidated Chippewa Agency, Duluth, Minnesota.

Dorothy McNulty, supervisor, nursery school, White Earth, Minnesota.

Charles Morrison, supervisor, White Earth Reservation division of the social and economic survey of 1934, Naytahwaush, Minnesota.

Adelle Northrup, R.N., state nurse, division of child welfare, State Department of Health, White Earth Reservation.

Abraham Pressman, M.D., superintendent, White Earth Hospital, White Earth Reservation.

Elizabeth Rowlette, clerk, division of statistics, Consolidated Chippewa Agency, Duluth, Minnesota.

Benno Watrin, O.S.B., missionary, Ponsford, White Earth Reservation.

Veronica Wieber, R.N., Minnesota state Chippewa health unit, Cass Lake, Minnesota.

Eugene Zeman, U.S. social worker, White Earth Reservation.

CHAPTER III

Housing Conditions
of One Hundred Fifty
Chippewa Families

A home, usually, is a dwelling where members of a family have a feeling of belonging, a feeling of security; where they exchange affections, sympathy, and kindness. It is a place where the great function of procreation has a privileged place; where life, once bestowed, is nourished; where minds and souls are trained in judgments, values, and controls according to the norm set by the adults within the home.

The material used in the construction of a dwelling, probably, has little effect upon it as a home. Dwellings may be of stone, such as are the New England homes; of brick or of planed lumber, as are the homes in the north-central part of our country; of mud, like some of the homes on the western prairies; of adobe, as among the Pueblo Indians; of poles and mud, as are the hogan of the Navaho; or of poles and bark, as were those of the early Chippewa. A dwelling is a home if it houses a family.

HISTORY OF HOUSING AMONG THE CHIPPEWA

The principal types of dwellings among the Chippewa, in the early days, were the wigwam, the peaked lodge, the bark house, and the tipi. After the coming of the white man, the Chippewa began to build log houses, tar-paper shacks, and frame houses, retaining the wigwam, however, for summer use. Indians returning from a trip could easily identify the home of fellow tribesmen. "We fellows could always tell an Indian's home from a white man's by the wigwam, and in more recent times by the canvas tent, found in the front yard of his home." Although today most Chippewa live in tar-paper shacks and frame houses, several types of the earlier dwellings are found on nearly all of their reservations.

THE WIGWAM

When the white man first came among the Chippewa, the latter made their homes in dome-shaped dwellings called wigwams. Wigwams were of two types, circular and elongated. In the making of a wigwam, saplings—usually peeled ironwood—were securely driven into the ground. If a circular wigwam was desired, the poles were placed in a circle; if an elongated one was needed, they were placed in an oval form.[1] Miss Densmore recorded a detailed account of the building of a wigwam. The description was given to her by a woman on the White Earth Reservation who was both builder and owner of it:

This wigwam was 12 ft. long and 10 ft. wide, with an entrance at one end. It was on slightly sloping ground, and a shallow ditch was dug across the back terminating half way down each side, to carry off the water in case of rain. The frame consisted of slender poles (3 on each side) set in the longer diameter, and 8 poles (4 on each side) set in the shorter diameter of the lodge. The poles on the longer diameter were about 38 inches apart, and on the shorter diameter about 14 inches apart. These poles were of ironwood, which is pliable when green and tough yet elastic when dry; thus it was possible to make a secure lodge of poles an inch or less in thickness. The poles were stuck firmly in the ground, those on the longer diameter being implanted first and the ends twisted together overhead, the length of the poles being such that the arch formed by them was about 5 feet above the ground at its highest point. The poles at the end of the lodge were then implanted and their ends similarly twisted, the overlapping portion being 1 to 1 feet. The intersections of the two parts of the frame were then tied with freshly cut strips of the inner bark of the basswood tree. The lengthwise and crosswise supports having been placed in position, 2 similar ironwood poles were arranged around the sides of the lodge, the lower of these being about 4 feet from the ground, and the other about 3 feet higher. These encircling poles were fastened around the erect framework, each intersection being tied with basswood bark. At one end of the lodge an opening was left in the lower of these braces for the doorway. The framework having been completed, the sides, except the doorway, were covered with bulrush mats. The woven edge of the mats was placed at the top, and tied to the framework; the rushes at the other edge of the mat, not being fastened together, had enough "spring" to assist in holding the mat upright.

In the lodge herein described a second row of mats was fastened to the framework about 18 inches above the ground on the windy side; affording protection from a possible draft. For additional warmth in winter, a second row of mats was frequently placed around the entire lodge overlapping the first row. The top of the lodge was covered with rolls of birch bark. These rolls were commonly about 10 or 12 feet long, and consisted of sheets of birch bark placed side by side, and sewed together with narrow strips of basswood bark. The ends were finished with sticks, which prevented the tearing of the bark, and made it possible to roll the material. The rolls of bark were laid first across the shorter diameter of the lodge, a space about 2 feet wide being left in the middle for the smoke hole. Short braces were placed between the lengthwise poles to support the inner edges for the birch bark, adjacent to the smoke hole. The rolls of birch bark were then laid on the longer diameter, leaving an opening for the smoke hole. The corners of the rolls were firmly secured by means of strips of bark passed between the rushes of the side walls, and tied to the framework of the lodge. These rolls were further held in place by strips of basswood bark sufficiently long to extend entirely over the lodge from side to side. These strips were usually secured to stakes, or to a longitudinal pole on each side. In this lodge, however, the strips of bark were wrapped around heavy stones which rested on the ground at either side of the lodge.[2]

The circular wigwam housed only one family, while the elongated gave shelter to as many as four. The sizes of both types varied. Bushnell describes one as being eighteen feet in length, and between eight and nine feet in width. Miss Densmore's was twelve feet long and ten and a half feet wide.[3] One found on the Lac Courte Orielle Reservation in 1935 was sixteen feet long, nine feet wide and seven feet high.

All work required in building a wigwam was done by the women except that of driving the poles into the ground, bending them, and holding them in position while they were being tied. Frameworks for wigwams were left in camping places and used annually during the seasonal occupation, but the coverings of birch-bark rolls and bulrush mats were carried by the women from place to place, as the seasonal food-gathering required.

Traditionally, the entrance to the wigwam was covered with a hide; in more recent times, the hide has been replaced by a blanket. The upper end of the covering was fastened to the wigwam, while the lower was weighted with a heavy stick or pole fastened horizontally near the ground end. If the wind blew too strongly through the regular entrance, the rush mats on the opposite side were loosened so as to permit entrance there.

The only wigwam of the earliest type–that in which birch-bark rolls and bulrush mats were used–that came to the writer's notice had been constructed and was owned by the wife of an old man on the Lac Courte Orielle Reservation, the keeper of the Midē wiwin drums and guardian of the frame-work of the Midē wiwin lodge. The wigwam coincided in nearly all details with that described by Miss Densmore.

However, in the building of most wigwams, in more recent times, rush mats and birch bark have been replaced by barks of other trees. One reason for the replacement is that it is difficult to find large birch trees from which wide strips of birch bark can be obtained. Elm, ash, tamarack, and Norway-pine barks are usually used as substitutes. At times it is difficult, too, to supply the bulrush mats. Consequently, today wigwams are found in which either the walls of bulrush mats or the roof of birch bark have been replaced by the rough bark of other trees; at times both walls and roof have been so replaced.

Several wigwams of the more recent type were found in blueberry patches on the Red Lake Reservation in 1932. The lower section of the walls of one of these, the part traditionally covered with bulrush mats, was covered with the bark of black ash. The upper section of the walls and the roof, the sections formerly covered with birch bark, were covered with the barks of Norway pine and black ash; the top and upper sides were covered with only the bark of Norway pine. The lower bark was tied to the framework with basswood fiber, while the roof was kept in place by being weighted down with a network of twine ropes at the end of which, about six feet from the ground, poles were fastened as weights. This particular wigwam was twelve feet in diameter and eight feet in height. Another wigwam in the same blueberry patch, an elongated one, was sixteen feet long, twelve feet wide, and eight feet high. Its lower walls were of bark of black ash; the top and upper sides were of birch bark. Each wigwam had an entrance about three feet wide and six feet high. None of the wigwams had smoke holes, cooking undoubtedly having been done out-of-doors over open fires, for tripods, cinders, and flat stones—the latter used in shutting off the wind—were in evidence near by. In the interior were platforms of lumber, elevated about a foot from the ground, which served as beds.

Mrs. Peter Everywind of Red Lake was using a wigwam for a storage house in 1932. She herself had built it. The walls were of bark of the black ash, and the roof, of that of the cedar tree. The interior upper ends had been prettily cut in zigzag pattern. "I wanted it to look nice on the inside," she said. "I built it well in every way, and I haven't had to repair it since I built it, way back in 1922."

Wigwams were seen on the White Earth Reservation in the summer of 1938, several of them being used by families included in this study. Two families were occupying one as a dwelling during the spring Midē wiwin at Ponsford. Its framework, twelve by sixteen by six feet in height, was of ironwood saplings and the roof was of birch bark. The traditional bulrush mats, however, had been replaced by old blankets and pieces of calico. Eight poles laid against the outside weighted down the bark.

From the center of the roof a stove pipe protruded, and an old blanket served as a door.

Skeletal frameworks of four other wigwams were found near homes. Three of these were in the wild-rice area near Rice Lake and were used by relatives of the owners during wild-rice season. It was interesting to note that all three, although entirely exposed to the weather, were used as storage places during the summer. Two were nearly filled with birch-bark rolls and with implements used in wild-rice gathering and maple-sugar making; the third contained wash tubs and firewood.

A fourth one, seen in the Ponsford area, was in the process of construction. A thirty-year-old woman noted that she had completed the framework and had the birch-bark rolls for the roofing ready, but that she lacked the bulrush mats. Her mother, fifty-two years of age, had in mind to make these. The wigwam was for her aged grandparents, a grandfather probably one hundred years old and a grandmother nearly that. They had complained so many times that they were uncomfortable in their tar-paper shack. It was hot in summer and cold and full of bedbugs in winter. And she added, "The old man says before the whites came, the Chippewa had no bedbugs nor smallpox nor tuberculosis!" It is interesting to note that Chippewa who were constructing, occupying, or owning wigwams in the summers of 1932, 1933, 1935, and 1938 were members of the Midē wiwin.

Although bark wigwams were found on all Chippewa reservations visited, few were intended for all-year-round dwellings. If found near homes, they were used for sleeping purposes during the summer months, or possibly as storage places. Those found scattered in berry patches, in sugar bushes, along lake shores where wild rice is gathered, and in places where the Midē wiwin is held, were occupied only seasonally. Wherever found, however, their general construction conformed closely to Miss Densmore's description.

THE PEAKED LODGE

Miss Densmore in writing of the peaked lodge records that it, "like the wigwam, consisted of a frame of poles covered with bark, but the structure instead of being dome-shaped, had a long ridge-pole and flat sides that sloped to the ground. Sheets of elm or cedar bark like those used on the 'bark houses' were placed on the sides of this lodge. Birch-bark rolls were similarly used . . ."[4] The lodges were long enough to permit three or four fireplaces, thereby accommodating three or four families. Smoke holes were not provided for, however, since the crossing of the poles left sufficient opening for the emission of smoke. Each end was provided with an entrance. The material used as covering was that which was familiar to the Chippewa in the building of their wigwams.

Bushnell photographed a peaked lodge in northern Minnesota in 1899.[5] Miss Densmore photographed a similar one at Grand Portage, Minnesota, in 1905.[6] The writer did not see a peaked lodge on any of the five Chippewa reservations covered in ethnological studies, nor was any seen on the White Earth Reservation. The question has been raised in her mind as to whether the shape of the peaked lodge was an adaptation of the gabled roof seen on the log houses of the white fur traders in the area. Informants on the White Earth Reservation were unable to give any information as to its origin or age.

THE BARK HOUSE

The material used in the making of a bark house was not unlike that used in the building of a wigwam. The framework consisted of poles of either ironwood or elm, the covering for both walls and roof being bark of either birch, elm, cedar, or Norway pine. The shape of the house, however, differed from the wigwam. Instead of bending the saplings so as to form a dome-shaped roof, they were permitted to stand upright like the walls of a house, with the framework of a low ridged roof resting on them.

The bark house, therefore, was not unlike a one-room dwelling with gabled roof. A man, aged ninety-six, who came to the White Earth Reservation previous to the days of the saw mill related that at his coming the Indians nearly all lived in bark houses.

The framework for several bark houses were seen by the writer on the White Earth Reservation in the wild-rice camps on Rice Lake in 1938.

THE TIPI

The tipi consisted of a conical framework of poles covered with long strips of birch bark so arranged that each top layer overlapped the one below it thus shedding the rain. The bark was fastened to the poles with basswood fiber and kept in place by being weighted down with leaning poles. The junction of the framework of the poles permitted the egress of smoke.

The tipi was undoubtedly borrowed from the plains tribes. One informant remarked, "Every Chippewa woman in the old days had to learn how to build a wigwam; it was part of the training her mother gave her.

None, however, knew how to build a tipi except those that had lived near the Sioux." Several tipis were seen on the Lac du Flambeau Reservation in 1935. Two of the tar-paper shack families of this study who participated in a pageant given at Itasca State Park in the summers of 1936 and 1937 owned tipis. Both had erected theirs near their tar-paper shack in the summer of 1938 and were using them for sleeping purposes.

THE LOG HOUSE

The first log houses that the Chippewa saw were the trading posts of the early fur traders. None, however, seem to have been built by them until the loggers who came into northern Minnesota built logging camps. Lumberjacks availing themselves of the heavy timber at hand found no difficulty in constructing comparatively warm houses. They felled large pine trees, peeled them of bark, and notched them at ends so they could be dovetailed and fitted to form nearly airtight walls. Crevices were chinked with moss and clay. Roofs, slightly gabled, were constructed by placing poles side by side and covering them with overlapping bark. Indian men of the timber area, working at logging with the whites, learnt their construction; Indian women, often married to white loggers, lived in them.

It does not appear, however, that log cabins became a favorite type of all-year-round dwelling for the Chippewa. They preferred passing their summers in the wigwams. Gilfillan wrote in 1901, "In 1873 nearly all the Ojibways everywhere, except the few newly removed to White Earth, lived winter and summer in birch bark wigwams. Now, nearly all of them have built for themselves, or have had built for them by the United States Government, one-roomed log cabins, in which they winter; but, in front of these, nearly every family puts up in summer an old style birch-bark wigwam, in which they pass the summer, returning to the log house when the cold weather sets in. They properly prefer the wigwam for its greater coolness, better circulation of air and greater cleanness. There are still, however, some families who from preference winter in birch-bark wigwams."[7] Most Chippewa at this time were still food gatherers, and food had to be found in several places. Log cabins could not be moved; rush mats and birch bark of the wigwam, on the contrary, could be packed on one's back and carried wherever desired.

TAR-PAPER SHACKS

Soon after the treaty of 1906, lands which had been ceded by the Chippewa were opened to homesteaders, and with them, it seems, tar-paper shacks entered the area. A homesteader was required to live on his land five successive years in order to make good his claim. Tar-paper shacks served well for the summer months of his residence, the severe winter months usually being spent in warmer quarters. Construction of a tar-paper shack was inexpensive and loss of it could not be great. Old Indians on the reservation recalled distinctly the first tar-paper shack they saw. "The farmers around here were the first ones to live in them," they said. The Indians, it seemed, did not begin building them until the late nineties. It was at that time that the United States Government distributed tar paper among them. "I remember well when my father brought home the first tar paper we ever had; the Indian agent was giving it out to the Indians," said a middle-aged woman.

A typical tar-paper shack as found on the White Earth Reservation consisted of a one-story framework of studding, the exterior of which was covered with rough one-inch boards of various widths. The cheapest lumber was usually gotten for covering, many times the first slats in the cutting of lumber being used. In several cases wooden boxes, used in shipping groceries and other supplies, were broken down and utilized. The boards, after being nailed to the studding, were covered with tar paper, the latter being securely fastened with narrow slats of wood or disks of tin. The extent to which wind and rain were kept from penetrating depended upon the condition of the paper.

Although the above was a typical tar-paper shack, two other types were seen on the reservation. In one type, the lumber of the typical shack was replaced by poles of smaller trees, these being conveniently available on land near the home. Only the windward side of the house, in this instance, was covered with tar paper. Such shacks were usually found in isolated regions. Another type of tar-paper shack was merely a frame house covered with tar paper. The house, probably built in boom days, was badly in need of repair, but since the owner was unable to purchase lumber he used tar paper in its repairing.

The roof of the tar-paper shack was usually a low-pitched, gabled one having varying degrees of slope. In a few instances it was shed-type, sloping in one direction only. It was generally covered with tar paper, although occasionally one was found with roofing of rubberoid or asphalt or even of shingles.

Chimneys on tar-paper shacks consisted of stove pipes of various lengths. These protruded through the roof directly over the kitchen stove or heater. The number of stove-pipe chimneys usually signified the number of rooms in the house. Pieces of tin were nailed to the roof about the stove-pipe projection to exclude the rain.

Framework for doors and windows were generally homemade. Doors, too, were ordinarily homemade, consisting of boards covered with tar paper.

Windows were of any conceivable size. They were commonly of half-size, however, and were removable, being held in position only by nails. Some were adjustable by sliding, and some opened on hinges. When double windows were used they were usually in a horizontal position, the height of the buildings not permitting a vertical one.

The walls of the interior often consisted of studding and of the rough unfinished lumber of the outside walls. In some cases the studding was covered with red rosin building paper or with broken down paste-board cartons; more often studdings and boards were pasted over with newspapers. The ceiling was sometimes covered with red rosin paper or paste-board cartons but more frequently it was unfinished, the bare joists and roof being visible.

An addition to the house was easily made and, therefore, a second, or even a third room, was often added. The added room might be an extension of the house and have the general appearance of the first room, or it might be a mere lean-to, a shed-like addition, with roof slanting in only one direction. The finish of the interior differed little from that of the other rooms.

A tar-paper shack had no foundation unless it was one of logs of one-log depth. Usually the flooring was nailed to the studdings on which the framework of the house rested. The ground was levelled so that the floor did not touch it in any place. Dogs often housed under floors, having easy access in many places in the summer, while in the winter but one entrance was left for them, the rest being closed up for the sake of warmth with a wide strip of tar paper which was held in place with a banking of earth or dung.

Entrances to tar-paper shacks consisted of low platforms, somewhat wider than the doors, or of a few boards or flat stones resting on the ground.

Although tar-paper shacks do not resemble wigwams in appearance, they do offer similar convenience in construction. They are built with little difficulty and, if forced by necessity, can be taken apart and moved to a new place in a manner not unlike the wigwams. It is significant, too, that both wigwams and a large number of the tar-paper shacks were one-room dwellings.

FRAME HOUSES

Lumber mills followed the logging camps, and with them, frame houses entered the area. The frame houses used by the Chippewa on the White Earth Reservation differed in no way from those used by their white neighbors. These houses ordinarily consisted of studding covered with rough boards not unlike those used in tar-paper shacks, the outside being covered with siding, however. The interior of some were finished with laths and covered with plaster, while others were covered with rosin paper or left unfinished. Roofs were of wooden shingles or of tar paper; chimneys were of brick or of stove pipe.

U.S. REHABILITATION HOUSES

In June 1937, the U.S. Bureau of Indian Affairs opened for occupancy forty houses constructed on the old U.S. agency farm in White Earth village. These were one-, two-, three-, or four-room, shingle-roofed frame houses built on concrete foundations. All had brick chimneys and roofed porches, several porches being screened. They varied in type, style, and arrangement. The interior walls which were seven to eight feet in height were finished in vertical sheathing and stained in gray and green; the ceilings were of press-board. All doors were panelled wood. Outside doors and all windows were screened.*

SEVENTY-ONE TAR-PAPER SHACKS**

Seventy-one of the one hundred fifty families lived in tar-paper shacks. Five of the shacks included in the seventy-one did not fall strictly under the typical shack as previously described in this study. They were log cabins, but were so badly damaged that nearly the entire exterior wall was covered with tar paper in order to give protection against the weather.

Sizes of the shacks varied, and none of them had an upstairs. Five of the buildings, however, had attics sufficiently high and with windows so that they were being used for sleeping rooms. The modal height–that of twenty-eight shacks–was eight feet. Table I indicates the sizes of the shacks.

*See Appendix F for illustrations of housing conditions of the one hundred fifty families.
**See Appendix C for complete tabular summary on housing conditions of the one hundred fifty families.

TABLE I

Sizes of Seventy-one Tar-paper Shacks on the White Earth Reservation in 1938

	PER CENT*
One-room shacks	50
Two-room shacks	31
Three-room shacks	17
Four-room shacks	2
Total	100

Typical small one-room shacks ranged in air space from 630 cubic feet (9x10 by 7 feet in height) to 840 (10x14 by 6 feet in height). Typical large one-room shacks contained 3240 (18x20 by 9 feet in height) and 3840 cubic feet (20x24 by 8 feet in height). The largest shack in the group, a three-room one, contained a total of 5940 cubic feet of air space. It consisted of a bedroom (15x18 by 8 feet in height), a bedroom dining-room of the same dimensions, and a dining-room kitchen (12x15 by 9 feet in height).

Some facts relative to the exterior of the homes are given in Table II.

TABLE II

Description of the Exterior of Seventy-one Tar-paper Shacks
on the White Earth Reservation in 1938

	PER CENT
Roof	
Tar paper	92
Wooden shingles	8
Total	100
Foundation	
None: buildings rested on ground	99
Logs of one-log depth	1
Total	100
Chimney	
Stove pipe	98
Brick	2
Total	100

*Throughout this work, in the use of percentages, figures equal to or greater than .5 are counted as 1; those less than .5, as 0.

TABLE II *(continued)*

	PER CENT
Porches	
One- or two-step platform	81
Boards, flat stone, or earth	19
Total	100
Doors	
Panelled and factory-made	52
Rough lumber and homemade	48
Total	100
Windows	
Homes with broken windows	23
Screens	
Homes with all windows screened	85
Homes with all outside doors screened	50

Brick chimneys were found only on the log houses. Stove-pipe chimneys in all cases led directly from the stoves to the roofs; in no case was an elbow used. This may have been for the sake of economy or it may have been a carry-over from wigwam days, fire in wigwams always being directly under the smoke hole.

The floor space of the one- or two-step platforms used as entrances varied in size from nine to thirty-six square feet. The homemade doors consisted of rough lumber held together by narrower boards nailed horizontally across them. Many of these doors were covered with tar paper.

Broken sections of windows were either covered with cardboard, stuffed with old clothes, or left uncovered. The seventy-one shacks had 162 full-sized, 104 half-sized, and 47 less than half-sized, unbroken windows. The homes gave the impression that, in general, they were well lighted and well aired.

Ten homes were without any window screens while two had some windows screened. The absence of screens is significant when one considers that mosquitoes are exceedingly troublesome at night during the greater part of the summer throughout the lake regions of Minnesota. In the twelve homes not protected by screens, mosquito netting was either spread over a framework of poles attached to the bed, or fastened to the rafters and permitted to hang over the sides of the bed. In two instances old blankets replaced the netting. In some homes a commercial mosquito spray was used at retiring and again at sunrise "when mosquitoes leave and flies start bothering one. Whoever is bothered most gets up and sprays the house."

The following table gives findings relative to the interior of the homes.

TABLE III

Facts Related to Height, Interior Walls, and Doors of Seventy-one Tar-paper Shacks on the White Earth Reservation in 1938

	NUMBER OF HOUSES
Height of rooms	
Five feet	2
Six feet	11
Seven feet	10
Eight feet	28
Nine feet	13
Ten feet	5
Fourteen feet	2
Total	71
Doorways	
Open passages	23
Cloth hangings	2
Doors of lumber	1

	PER CENT
Wall finishings	
Unfinished	43
Rosin paper	46
Lumber	5
Painted or white washed	5
News- or wrapping papers or wall paper	1
Total	100

The unfinished interior walls consisted of the studding and rough boards that formed the outside walls. In the homes where these were covered with newspaper, wrapping paper, or wall paper, the paper was pasted or tacked directly on the lumber. The paper merely served to make the walls look cleaner; they had become dark and unattractive-looking due to smoke and age. It was not uncommon to see walls covered with a conglomerate assortment of sheets of the St. Paul *Pioneer*

Press, Ladies Home Journal, St. Anthony Messenger, Love and Romance, Sunday Visitor, comic sheets of the Chicago *Tribune,* photogravure of the Minneapolis *Tribune,* grocery sacks, and wrapping papers. One housewife had used wall paper of a pretty color and design. When rosin paper was used it was tacked taut over the studding and joists, thus forming an air space between it and the outer lumber. None of the walls of the homes was plastered.

The construction of a tar-paper shack—one that conformed closely to type and consisted of one room (14x14 by 6 feet in height) and a lean-to (9x12 by 6 feet in height)—cost $27.86. Sadie,* mother of the family, and her husband, George, had built it in the fall of 1936 with money earned by the sale of wild rice which they had gathered. The studding for the house cost $5.00; lumber for walls, $8.00; flooring, $6.00; and five windows at $1.00 each, $5.00. The door, its frame, and the window frames were homemade. One door knob and two hinges cost $.65; nails, $.50. Two rolls of blue rosin paper used on inside walls cost $1.96, and tacks used in attaching the paper to studdings, $.75. Sadie's cousin hauled the material in his truck, the couple merely paying for the gas. Early in the spring of 1938, Sadie's sister, Mary, found employment on the W.P.A. project. In order that she might be near her work and be able to bring the persons whom she was supporting with her, namely her mother and brother and her illegitimate child, Sadie and George allowed Mary to occupy their shack. They themselves moved into a smaller one, one that was on the land when they were given permission to occupy it. The shack was badly in need of reconstruction. They expected that tar paper for the exterior repairing of three walls (12x14 by 7 feet) would cost $2.50; three rolls of roofing would cost $2.75; rosin paper for the interior, $1.25; a total, therefore, of $6.50. When the above had been done and all exterior sides of the shack had been banked to a height of three feet from the ground, the house would be in readiness for four or five months of sub-zero weather; even for weather when it took a dip of 50° below zero.

The upkeep of Mrs. Thunder's one-room tar-paper shack was probably typical of many others. She bought her shack, a house 12x24 by 7 feet in height, seven years ago, paying $25.00 for it. Since then she had covered the exterior once every two years at a cost of $11.00—the tar paper required for the walls amounting to six rolls at $7.50 and the roofing, to two rolls at $3.50. The repairing of the interior required two rolls of rosin paper each year at $2.00. The yearly upkeep, therefore, averaged

---

*All names referring to persons are fictitious.

$7.50, plus an additional cost for nails, the amount depending upon the number of old nails that were useable.

SEVENTY-ONE FRAME HOUSES

Frame houses in general were larger than were tar-paper shacks. Thirty-nine of them had the semblance of a second story, windows, however, being found at gable ends since side walls were too low. Twenty-two had attics. Table IV indicates the sizes of the frame houses.

TABLE IV

Sizes of Seventy-one Frame Houses on the White Earth Reservation in 1938

	PER CENT
One-room houses	3
Two-room houses	30
Three-room houses	30
Four-room houses	16
Five-room houses	9
Six-room houses	4
Seven-room houses	4
Eight-room houses	3
Nine-room houses	1
Total	100

Frame houses varied greatly in air space. A one-room house (10x12 by 6 feet in height) contained 720 cubic feet. A two-room house (6x9 and 12x12 and 6 feet in height) contained 1188 cubic feet. A four-room house contained 10,368 cubic feet. It consisted of a dining-room kitchen (16x18 by 6 feet in height), of a living-room and two bedrooms (each 18x20 by 8 feet in height).

Some findings descriptive of the exterior of the buildings are given in Table V.

TABLE V

Description of the Exterior of Seventy-one Frame Houses
on the White Earth Reservation in 1938

	PER CENT
Roofs	
Tar paper	28
Wooden shingles	72
Total	100

TABLE V *(continued)*

	PER CENT
Foundation	
None: buildings resting on ground	53
Logs	–
Stone	14
Cement	33
Total	100
Chimney	
Stove pipe	44
Brick	56
Total	100
Porches	
Boards, flat stones, or earth	7
One- or two-step platforms	86
Screened	7
Total	100
Doors	
Rough lumber and homemade	13
Panelled and factory-made	87
Total	100
Windows	
Homes with broken windows	31
Screens	
Homes with all windows screened	99
Homes with all outside doors screened	80

Several of the houses had both stove-pipe and brick chimneys. In such homes the stove pipe was usually found leading from a stove in a lean-to used as a kitchen. Homemade doors were like those found in the tar-paper shacks. Broken sections of windows presented the same appearance as did those of the shacks. The seventy-one frame houses had 376 full-sized windows, 41 half-sized, and 14 less than half-sized. Families that were not protected from insects by screens used netting at night suspending it from rafters and spreading it over the edges of the beds or letting it rest on poles fastened to the beds.

In general, the interior of the frame houses showed greater advancement than did the interior of the tar-paper shacks. Table VI gives findings relative to the interior.

TABLE VI

Findings Relative to Height, Interior Walls, and Doors of Seventy-one
Frame Houses on the White Earth Reservation in 1938

	NUMBER OF HOUSES
Height of rooms	
Six feet	5
Seven feet	10
Eight feet	34
Nine feet	10
Ten feet or more	12
Total	71
Doorways	
Open passages	21
Cloth hangings	1
Rough lumber	19
Panelled	129
Wall finishings	
Unfinished	8
Rosin paper	31
Lumber	16
Composition board	2
Paint or whitewash	24
Plaster	19
Wall paper	1

EIGHT UNITED STATES REHABILITATION HOUSES

Eight of the forty rehabilitation houses located in the village of White
Earth were included in this study. They were not in any way typical of
housing conditions of the Indians on the White Earth Reservation.
Since, however, forty such homes were occupied by Indian families
whose living conditions economic resources, and social status was like
that of families generally spoken of as Indian families, it was thought fair
to include eight of them.

Two of the eight houses consisted of two rooms, five of three rooms,
and one of four rooms. Four had upstairs which were being used for
sleeping purposes. All houses being new were in good repair.

Air space in the homes varied with the number of rooms. The height
of rooms was either 6 or 8 feet and floor space either 8x12 feet or 12x15
feet. The two two-room houses each contained 2880 cubic feet, each

having a bedroom living-room and dining-room kitchen (each room being 12x15 feet and all rooms being 8 feet in height). The four-room house contained 5040 cubic feet and consisted of two bedrooms (each 12x15 by 6 feet in height), of a living-room and of a dining-room kitchen (each 12x15 by 8 feet in height).

OWNERSHIP OF HOMES

TAR-PAPER SHACKS

Of the tar-paper shacks fifty-five (seventy-seven per cent) were owned by persons living in them, while in five others occupants were making payments. Sixty families then, or approximately eighty-five per cent, had vested interests in their homes. The remaining eleven were either renters or free occupants. In forty-one of the sixty families who had vested interests in homes, parents owned the home jointly; in six, the mother alone, she having built it with money she had earned. In two cases it belonged to minor children, in one instance a widowed father having built it for his ten-year-old son in order that the latter and his grandmother might live there; and in the other, a mother, married a second time, built one for the minor children of her first marriage, using their 1935 annuity payments. Four couples lived in shacks built by grandparents, the latter feeling in two cases that their married granddaughter should be given a start in life; while in the other two cases, grandparents knew the grandchild would care for them in their old age. In the remaining seven cases the shack belonged to some blood relative who was considered a member of the family.

Although all families were certain of the ownership, or non-ownership, of their shacks, they were not all certain of the ownership of the land on which it stood since delinquent taxes might have reverted it to the state. Seven owned the land and had paid the taxes. Eleven others were certain that they had owned the land at one time but were not certain whether delinquent taxes had not deprived them of it. Four families lived on original allotments, one on his own and three others on inherited lands.

The eleven renters owned neither shack nor land. The rent they were paying varied from $2.00 to $5.00 per year. Thirty-eight of the families owned their shacks but not the land: Sixteen of these had built on United States Government lands, two on Methodist church property, and twenty on the land of white owners from whom they had gotten permission to squat. In some cases they used the lake shore for fishing and some land for gardening.

None of the tar-paper shacks was insured and none of the shacks nor any of the land was mortgaged.

FRAME HOUSES

Twenty-six (thirty-six per cent) of the dwellers in frame houses either owned both land on which it stood, or they lived with an aged relative who owned both house and land. Seven owned their homes but not the land, having built on U.S. Government land. Thirty-eight owned neither land nor home: six living in government homes on United States Government land; twenty-eight renting their homes, rent ranging from $2.00 to $10.00 a year; and four being tolerated in the homes in which they lived because no one cared for the houses.

Three of the frame-house dwellers had lost the land upon which their houses stood because of delinquent taxes; taxes were delinquent on eight others. Three homes and the land on which they stood were mortgaged and payments were not being met. One of the frame houses was insured against fire.

REHABILITATION HOUSES

Dwellers in the rehabilitation houses were all meeting their quarterly payments ranging from $11.00 to $17.00. The price of the homesteads varied with the size of the building, the accessories in the place, and the number of acres belonging to it. One hundred equal payments, paid quarterly, will pay for the entire homestead in twenty-five years. Any amount, however, can be paid at any time. When all payments have been made, the land and buildings will belong to the owner and to his blood heirs. As property of the United States it cannot be taxed, sold, or mortgaged. If unoccupied for twelve months it becomes tribal property.

A committee of five Chippewa men and women, who are elected each year, select the families to whom the houses are assigned. Families selected were such as gave promise of keeping up buildings, property, and payments. Since the opening of the homes one family had vacated a house voluntarily, while another, because of non-payment, had been asked to leave it.

CONCLUSIONS

A significant finding in connection with ownership of homes is that sixty, or approximately eighty-five per cent, of those who lived in tar-paper shacks owned their homes, while only thirty-three, or approximately forty-seven per cent, of those who lived in frame houses did.

ATTITUDE TOWARD PRESENT LOCATION OF HOMES

One or both parents in the one hundred fifty homes were asked this question: "Would you like to leave this home?" The answers revealed that those who owned their homes, no matter how dilapidated and inadequate the homes were, were quite unwilling to leave them.

ATTITUDE OF TAR-PAPER SHACK DWELLERS

Fifty-two (seventy-three per cent) of the occupants of tar-paper shacks were unwilling to leave their homes, while seven were willing to move; twelve were undecided.

The following answers are typical of the ones received from tar-paper shack occupants: Thirty-five-year-old Anna said, "No, I wouldn't like to move from here. I like it right here in this old shack. It's more like the old Indian ways and I like them best." Fifty-year-old Mary, while busily engaged in making a braided rug, remarked: "My husband was born right here and I have lived here with him and my children fifteen years. I'm well acquainted with all the woods and everything out here, and I wouldn't want to move."

Ella, a woman in the sixties, who was visiting her next door neighbor, Clara, a woman of her own age, answered, "It's just as good here as any place. This is my own shack and I feel at home here." Both women were busily engaged in the shade of some tall jack pine making birch-bark baskets "for a store that sells them to tourists." Clara answered, "I, too, like my place. I go away for a month every summer visiting relatives and I'm always glad to come back here."

A thirty-two-year-old man, owner of a shack of two small rooms, remarked, "No, we wouldn't like to leave this house; we own it. I don't like the location, however, and wish we could live away from other people, somewhere in the woods. We never did care to live amongst other people." He called our attention to the interior of his house which was attractively arranged, and continued, "I made all the furniture in here except the cabinet, and, of course, the stove! And my wife painted all of it." Both parents had completed first year high school; he at Pipestone, she at Callaway. Neither of them had been out of the state except to Fargo, North Dakota. They pointed with pride to a five-year-old son; and they wanted us to see the baby.

A widowed mother, sixty-one years of age, living on the outskirts of one of the highway towns was certain she would never leave her tar-paper shack. "My husband planted all these trees and they are like persons to me." Her household consisted of herself; her son, twenty-six; her divorced daughter and child; her granddaughter, twelve; and her aged uncle who had come to visit indefinitely. Her formal education consisted of one month at the Mission School at White Earth. Her son who had supported her for nearly five years was earning $44.00 a month on a W.P.A. job. Besides supporting his mother's entire household, he was paying on a fifty-dollar radio and was buying back the house and lot "which the taxes had ate up!" She thought she ought to use some of the money to buy herself some clothes so she could attend Mass on Sunday, but, on the other hand, she did not wish to deprive her son of some pleasure. "I can't take everything from him; he don't drink and that's lots to thank God for." They had no books, but they purchased the Mahnomen weekly newspaper occasionally. "Whenever we want to find out the truth about something, like about the Cass Lake Agency affair; and then about those worms!" (Army worms were destroying the crops between Mahnomen and Waubun.) "I haven't any worries now. My daughter was married by the justice of the peace and she and her husband were always scrapping. He didn't believe in children, and she wanted them. Now they are divorced, and I am glad."

Jim, forty years of age, and Ella, thirty-eight, wanted to stay in the old, ramshackled, tar-paper-covered log cabin. It belonged to his wife's mother, aged seventy, with whom they, their three preschool children and a ten-year-old son were making their home. "This house rattles dreadfully. We are scared that some day it will fall together. Last evening when we had that dreadful storm, we all got ready to get out. This house is fifty years old, but we want to stay here and have it fixed up." The old grandmother stopped eating her meal of venison stew, spaghetti, and baking-powder biscuits, and with the emphasis and decision that is so characteristic of the Chippewa of the old culture, said: "I'll stay right here. I won't leave here. I've lived here too long." She was a member of the Midē wiwin and had "grand medicine" in her possession. A fresh deer hide, sinews, and deer brain were drying while hanging across the rafters. She intended to tan hides soon and to make moccasins for winter use for herself, her daughter, and the three little ones. All were wearing them then. The baby had been lulled to sleep in a hammock made Chippewa fashion. Neither was Ella interested in moving into a rehabilitation house. "We'll stay right here with my mother. We are all right here, if only we can get the house fixed up!" Their income was $60.00 a month, her husband earning $45.00 at C.C.C.-I.D. and her mother receiving $15.00 old age assistance. Potatoes and corn were all they had planted in their one-acre garden. They owned no books but subscribed to the *Farmer's Wife* and purchased the St. Paul *Pioneer Press* from the "paper-man" on Sundays, "mostly so the kids have the funnies." Jim completed the third grade in Pipestone; Ella, the fourth at Wahpeton. Jim was Protestant; Ella, Catholic. Ella had been married to a man "Indian way" but left him fourteen years ago, and had lived with Jim in the same manner ever since. Both parents had voted at the state primary election and at the referendum vote held in June.

Old Man Mink, seventy-eight years of age, and his wife, ten years his junior, agreed that they liked their one-room shack. The old man had just returned from getting a pail of fish which a neighbor let him take from his net. "It's dangerous to fish around here; the game warden lives in this town," he remarked. He searched among the leaves in his pail where the fish were concealed, and offered us two fine half-alive rock bass. Then settling into his armchair while his wife squatted on the bed, he noted in a plaintive tired voice, "No, we don't want to leave here; we have been here so long now. We want to stay here. We might want to move if we were younger, but we have only a few more years to live. Sometimes we go away for a little visit but we always want to come back here again." His wife, in more youthful vigor, added, "Yes, we like it here; but that's not saying that we must stay here. If we ever feel like moving, we'll just up and move and go where we like it better." "I carried mail on rural route for twelve years," the old man interjected, "but eight years ago some fellow underbid me and I lost the route. I was then getting $1440.00 a year." "No, I haven't any money in the bank; never did have any there, nor have we any insurance. We get $30.00 old age pension a month now and we get along fine on that except for clothes. We have all our bills paid except for the plowing of our garden." His first two wives had died; he married his present wife a year ago after living with her in common-law marriage for seventeen years. He is Catholic; she, Episcopal. A twelve-year-old grandson who attends the district school in the village makes his home with them. They have no books in the home nor do they subscribe for or buy a newspaper. The husband had completed the fifth grade in a district school in Morrison County (a white community), while his wife had spent three years at the Girls' Indian School at St. Joseph, Minnesota.

The unwillingness of the tar-paper shack dwellers to leave their homes might have been expected since so large a number owned them. It was thought, however, that they might be quite willing to leave them to become occupants of the rehabilitation houses because of the latter's newness, their equipment, warmth, etc. The question, "Would you like to move into a rehabilitation house, one of those new homes built by the Government for Indians of the White Earth Reservation?" was therefore asked of one or both parents in each family. Answers revealed that sixty-six were unwilling to move into one of them: fifty-three, because they disliked the village of White Earth; nine, because the cost was too high; two, had free rent; two, because there was difficulty in getting water and wood in White Earth. Two were undecided not having seen the "new houses," while three were willing to move into them.

The following is illustrative of the families who were not interested in occupying a rehabilitation house. Mike, twenty-nine, Jane, twenty-eight, and their ten-year-old son lived in a one-room tar-paper shack neatly furnished and attractively arranged. She was a white woman and he, "a regular League of Nations" as he expressed it. "I'm on the roll, however, and that makes me an Indian," he added. "We could have had one of the rehabilitation houses but there is too much red tape connected with getting one. Anyway, there is nothing here in White Earth for which we'd want our children and children's children to stay! We are contented in our shack, for $44.00 W.P.A. wage feeds us, buys our clothes, pays our rent, and gets us a second-hand car. And we don't run any bills either!" Both parents had completed the eighth grade in day schools off the reservation. They had no space for gardening, but Jane canned more than one hundred quarts of vegetables last year, her mother sending her some vegetables whenever an opportunity presented itself. They moved from Detroit Lakes to White Earth in order that Mike might find employment with W.P.A. "As an Indian, my husband has privileges on the reservation," said Jane.

ATTITUDE OF FRAME-HOUSE DWELLERS

Of the seventy-one frame-house dwellers, twenty-two (thirty-one per cent) were unwilling to leave the house they were occupying; nine were undecided; forty were willing to leave.

Forty-six (sixty-five per cent) of the seventy-one frame-house occupants were unwilling to move into a United States rehabilitation house; twelve were undecided; seven were not even interested in thinking the matter over; six were willing to move into one.

Eleven of the forty-six who were unwilling to move into a rehabilitation house disliked White Earth village; three thought morals there were very bad. "Why weren't those buildings scattered over the reservation? I wouldn't live in White Earth if you gave me the entire town!" said one. Another: "Oh, no! Never to White Earth! It's the filthiest place on earth! Even small girls there go out with married men; I saw it myself." "White Earth has had a bad reputation for years. Why are they offering opportunities only to Indians who are willing to live there?" inquired a mother.

Nine of the forty-six who were unwilling to move into a rehabilitation house considered the cost too high. Various informants remarked: "Those White Earth houses cost too much. I'd like to own my own home right along, and not to be paying for it for so long a time." "It's really better here, only our house is in bad shape and I have an awful time keeping the bedbugs out. We may have to tear it down this fall and rebuild it, just to get rid of the bugs." "We like the rehabilitation houses all right, but don't think we could afford one." "We want a house of our own; not an expensive one, but one that we can fix up ourselves."

Two had free occupancy. Four knew there was difficulty in getting water and wood in White Earth. "We like our own home town. If some of those houses were out here we would consider taking one. We never could figure out why they didn't build some here where it's easy to get water and wood." "No, not out there in White Earth; it's too hard to get wood there. Out here we can get all the dry wood we need. Of course, if we are caught cutting green wood we're in for trouble."

ATTITUDE OF DWELLERS IN REHABILITATION HOUSES

Dwellers in the rehabilitation houses are willing to continue living in them, although some feared that they would be unable to make payments when government relief work is discontinued. "I couldn't leave here anymore; the houses I used to live in were like barns!" "I like a bigger house than the shacks I used to live in. This has three rooms and it's fine."

CONCLUSIONS

It was noticeable as one moved among the people on the reservation that contentment and congeniality was characteristic of some of the communities, while it was lacking in others. It was probably more than a coincidence that it existed in the areas where ownership of homes predominated, and owners of homes prevailed in the tar-paper shack group.

SOURCES

1. David I. Bushnell, Jr., *Ojibway Habitations and Other Structures* (In Annual Report of the Smithsonian Institution for the year ending June 30, 1917 [1919]), p. 609-613, *passim.*
   Joseph A. Gilfillan, *The Ojibways in Minnesota* (In Collections of the Minnesota Historical Society, IX [1901]), 55-128, *passim.*
   Laurence Oliphant, *Minnesota and the Far West* (Edinburgh and London: William Blackwood & Sons, 1855), p. 193-194.
   William Warren. *History of the Ojibways* (In Collections of the Minnesota Historical Society, V [1885]), 40, 100, 254.
2. Frances Densmore, *Chippewa Customs* (U.S. Bureau of American Ethnology Bulletin 86 [1929]), p. 23-24.
3. Bushnell, *op. cit.,* p. 613; Densmore, *op. cit.,* p. 23.
4. *Op. cit.,* p. 26.
5. David I. Bushnell, Jr., *Native Villages and Village Sites East of the Mississippi* (U.S. Bureau of American Ethnology Bulletin 69 [1919]), Plate 2.
6. *Op. cit.,* p. 26, Plate 5, b.
7. *Op. cit.,* p. 62.

CHAPTER IV

The One Hundred Fifty Chippewa Families

After finding that there is a positive relationship between tar-paper shacks and ownership, contentment, and geniality in the one hundred fifty families, one is interested in knowing *who* lives in these shacks? Why are they contented to be there? Is it because they own their homes? Is it because they are a group of the old generation who merely moved from wigwam to tar-paper shack and find the similarity comforting? Or are they people who were born on the reservation, who have had little formal education, no trade or professional training, and who, having seen little else than the reservation, are content to live as they do? Are they Grand Medicine people, living in common-law marriages, and speaking only Chippewa? Are they perhaps acting wisely by living in shacks whose building maintenance is cheap, since they are a group living on a subsistence level? Who lives in frame houses? Are the families who live in them the ones who speak English, who have had educational opportunities, who are members of the Christian religions, living up to Christian teachings?

AGE GROUPS OF PARENTS[*]

Our study revealed that when the parents of the one hundred fifty families were grouped into age groups of a generation—counting one-third of a century as a generation—the following occurred: Twenty-two per cent were of the first or oldest generation, the ones born between 1839 and 1872; fifty-one per cent of the second generation, the ones born between 1871 and 1905; and twenty-seven per cent of the third or present generation, the ones born since 1904.

---

[*]Tabulations under the various sub-headings of Chapter IV are found in Appendix D.

FIRST GENERATION

The twenty-two per cent forming the first generation included forty-six men and women, ranging in age from sixty-six to one hundred two years. Some of this group were in their teens in the days of treaties, land cessions, and first allotments–the ones of 1854. They were in their twenties and thirties, when the significant treaty of 1867 was signed, whereby the Chippewa ceded two million acres of land in return for which the U.S. Government promised to pay annuities, supply cattle, schools, houses, physicians' expenses, clothing and supplies. Furthermore, it was this treaty that set aside the White Earth Reservation. Many of this generation had reached maturity by 1887 when allotments of one hundred sixty acres were made to each Chippewa residing on the White Earth Reservation.

It is this group, also, that well remembers the days of the Treaty of 1889 whereby more land was ceded to the Government and more money deposited for them in the United States Treasury, the interest of which was to be paid to them and their heirs in annual per-capita payments, while one-fourth was to be used for educational purposes for their descendents. They were in full maturity in the days of timber sales of 1904 and allotment sales of 1906.

It was the first generation, then, that experienced the days of tribal ownership of vast tracts of land where hunting and fishing and making a living according to the traditional Chippewa way was comparatively easy. It was this group that lived to see its people, inexperienced in the handling of money and individual property, deprived, by white men's business tactics, of land, of fishing, and of hunting rights; it was this group that saw its people landless and property-less. Before recent government relief projects, they experienced with their own people the point of starvation.

It was the first generation, too, that in its youth had had the benefits of tribal social controls so effective in that day, and who taught them to their children, but who are saddened by the failure to persuade their grandchildren and great-grandchildren to accept them. In every community it is this group that more particularly laments the inroads that liquor and its concomitant evils have made into the second, and, especially, into the third generation.

This group, today, adheres with firm conviction and a good deal of independence to traditional tribal customs. They live in common-law marriage having been true to one spouse for fifty, sixty, seventy and more years, and urge their grandchildren of marriageable age to enter such marriages, "because those church marriages can't be broken and you'd better try each other out first." They are largely members of the Midē wiwin and speak only Chippewa. They harvest wild rice and parch it; gather maple sap and refine it; use medicinal herbs and roots and call on the Grand Medicine men in time of serious illness. They wear moccasins, sleep in day-clothes, and make their beds on the floor. They unhesitatingly say that modern education has been no substitute for traditional, parental training. They accept old age assistance graciously and with independence, since "It's what the Government promised us for our lands!" Twenty-five per cent of those who live in tar-paper shacks and twenty-eight per cent of the frame-house people belong to the first generation.

This group undeniably exists on the White Earth Reservation and is a factor in its culture. Insidiously, but blamelessly, its members prolong the traditional culture. They are most certainly implanting culture conflicts into the minds of the generation of grade-school age. At times grandparents live in homes where grandchildren live. Other old people, following their traditions, adopt, not legally but in "Chippewa way," one or two of their grandchildren. Grandchildren so adopted live their lives entirely under the influence of the grandparents. Contact in play and during leisure time with children at St. Benedict's Mission School of White Earth offered convincing evidence that many Chippewa children are learning the mental content of the old culture, as well as many of the external expressions of it. "My grandma has 'grand medicine' and everybody fears her!" says one. "My grandma can make it rain by blowing into bones in that direction (pointing west), just when the sun begins to go down. She did it twice this summer and both times it rained two days after!" says another. Many of the children had seen fire balls (marsh gas) and tell of its evil effects. "One moved along the shores of Round Lake last month and landed right in front of my cousin's house and the next morning he was sick, and he died three days after that!" Many similar comments are heard from grade children. These children play at cooking food in the open by hanging kettles from tripods. They wrap dolls like Chippewa mothers wrap their babies, and swing them to sleep in Chippewa-made hammocks. Using discarded tin pails for drums, they dance the Squaw Dance, the Rabbit Dance, and other Chippewa dances. Some can make birch-bark articles and willow baskets. Wild rice for dinner is a delight; and thorn apples are a picnic!

SECOND GENERATION

Fifty-one per cent of the parents of the one hundred fifty families were of the ages of the second generation. This was to be expected since mortality occurs more frequently in the first generation, and pre-adolescence is included in the third.

The greatest variation in culture pattern was found in the second generation. It was a portion of this generation, rather than of the first or the third, that showed the amalgamation of Chippewa and European civilization in its own pattern. It was in dealing with this group, too, that one realized that these Indians, in a comparatively few years, were expected to have absorbed centuries of European civilization. There were parents in the group, on the one hand, who still followed the old Chippewa pattern closely and who considered themselves Indians in every sense of the word. On the other hand, one found parents whose identity as Chippewa was only assured after consulting the tribal roll, for they were "pale-faces," indeed, and conformed to the European-American standard of living in every way. Between these extremes was the larger group which had compromised between the two patterns and was neither Chippewa nor white. They were Catholics or Episcopals or Methodists, but lived in common-law marriage. They gathered wild rice and parched it, but they cold-packed vegetables and meat, laughing at the idea of drying them like their mothers did. They spent W.P.A. money for liquor, and were paying by installments for a hundred-dollar console radio. They wore moccasins, slept in day-clothes in beds on deer-hair, feather or straw mattresses and without sheets and pillow slips. They wished to know the date of the next annuity payment! Most of this group spoke both Chippewa and English. Forty-eight per cent of the families living in tar-paper shacks and fifty-four per cent of those living in frame houses belonged to the second generation. Five of the eight families in the rehabilitation houses were also of this group.

THIRD GENERATION

Twenty-seven per cent of the parents in the one hundred fifty families were born since 1905, since the days of the last allotments. They are participants in tribal funds, but were never the recipients of allotments. If the roll indicates that they are a quarter-blood or more, they have not only the privilege of taking advantage of the educational tribal funds which are applicable to them when in attendance at U.S. Government or Mission boarding schools, but they may also make loans for advanced study.

Some of the third-generation parents of the one hundred fifty families had taken advantage of educational opportunities; others had not. Some kept good homes on a subsistence income; others lived on low standards in every way. Some retained tribal customs to a small degree; a few were members of the Midē wiwin. All spoke English; a few spoke Chippewa and many of them understood it. One marvelled at the extent to which, in this swift moving civilization, the third generation of a comparatively primitive culture had been able to adopt a highly complex one. Twenty-seven per cent of the families living in tar-paper shacks and eighteen per cent of those living in frame houses were of the third generation.

CONCLUSIONS

There was no significant relationship between housing and the first generation, and only a slight one between housing and the second generation, the number of the latter living in frame houses exceeding those living in tar-paper shacks by six per cent. Of the third generation, however, those living in tar-paper shacks exceeded the ones living in frame houses by nine per cent. The third generation not having received allotments has had only its current income and an occasional small annuity or per-capita payment to buy with and has probably found the tar-paper shack, rather than the frame house, within its purchasing power.

Of the eight families living in rehabilitation houses, three were of the present generation, and, as indicated before, five were of the second while none was of the first. Age alone would have barred the first generation from the houses since payments were beyond their income, most of them receiving old age assistance. Although the occupants of the rehabilitation houses were a selected group, and were expected to meet certain requirements, people living in them adhered to various standards. In fact, they differed in no significant particulars from the families found in frame houses.

MARITAL STATUS OF PARENTS

PRESENT MARRIAGES

The traditional culture pattern of the Chippewa had its accepted social form of marriage. A girl was of marriageable age at fourteen or fifteen, soon after she reached puberty, while a boy was only considered so when he had proven to the community that he was able to provide for a family. Bringing home several deer after a hunting expedition was sufficient evidence, a thing which boys were usually unable to do until they were in their twenties.

Parents and elders exercised a good deal of influence in the selection of mates. In fact, company keeping, except in the presence of elders, was taboo. There was no marriage ceremony and consequently no exchange of marriage vows; couples merely lived in common-law marriage. The Chippewa speak of it today as being married in "Indian way." The couple lived in the home of the girl's parents for a year after their marriage. If they were unable to live together agreeably and no pregnancy occurred, they merely parted, the man returning to his own parents. If, however, a child was born, the mother, shortly after the birth, erected her own wigwam and the couple set up individual housekeeping.

Separations were permitted. A man might merely leave his wife and children and continue to live in the community, or he might leave it and in time remarry. A woman, too, might leave her husband and children and return to her parents' home and in due time remarry.

Separations were, therefore, permitted and were an accepted thing in the community; not so infidelity on the part of the wife. It was expected that an unfaithful wife be punished by her husband. If he were lenient, he might merely cut off one of her braids; if he were infuriated and very jealous, he would cut off an ear or her nose, and no one in the community would chide him for it. Old Chippewa in the various communities on the White Earth Reservation, as well as on other Chippewa reservations, can give names of women who were so deformed and tell that in their fireside instructions they were told that this was the punishment dealt out to unfaithful wives.

The following quotation from one of the writer's unpublished manuscripts, dealing with the Chippewa, is based almost entirely on material found in the literature. All sources consulted are older than her own field notes, and most are corroborated by them:

> Moral standards of the Chippewa women of the early day were very high.[1] Immorality was rarely found among them for mothers kept their daughters near them and seldom allowed them to be out of sight. Girls were of marriageable age at fourteen or fifteen years.[2]
>
> A young man who wished to call on a young maiden talked first with the older people who lived next to her lodge. He then entered the girl's lodge and talked with the girl in a low tone. She was not, however, permitted to leave the lodge with him. If he happened to call late in the evening, and the embers were low, the mother or grandmother stirred up the fire so that it burnt brightly, filled her pipe, and sat up and smoked. The young man felt that he was being watched at all times. He might on an evening play his courting flute somewhere near the lodge, but the girl was never allowed to leave the lodge in response to it.[3] Mr. Thomas L. McKenney, when en route with Governor Lewis Cass in 1826, heard such

a flute and wrote: "Nothing can be more mournful in its tones. It was night, and a calm rested on everything; and it was moonlight, all of which added to its effect. We saw the Indian who was playing it, sitting on a rock. . . . We afterwards learned that this Indian was in love, and that he would sit there all night indulging in this sentimental method of softening the heart of his mistress, whose lodge he took care should be opposite his place of melody, and within reach of his monotonous but pensive strains."[4]

If a young man was serious in his intentions, he killed a deer or some other animal and brought it to the lodge of the girl's parents. This signified his intention of providing well for his family. Armstrong wrote in 1892: "Leaving it outside, he enters the wigwam, saying nothing, but lights his pipe and makes himself at home. Should there be more than one girl in the lodge at the time, he has a sign by which his choice is made known. If the girl does not like his appearance she remains where she is, but if he is agreeable to her fancy she takes a knife and proceeds to skin the animal and take charge of the meat, after which the suitor takes his leave. The parents of the girl, being advised of what is going on by the presence of the meat not of their killing, commence systematic proceedings to ascertain the young man's habits, his ability as a hunter, warrior, etc., and if satisfied with them they proceed to the young man's parents, who are now for the first time aware of the youth's aspirations and they in turn make inquiry as to the character, etc., of their prospective daughter-in-law. If all is satisfactory the young man is given permission by the girl's parents to visit her, but all he or she has to say must be said in the common wigwam and before all who happen to be present. If they become satisfied with each other and he has been able to convince her parents that he is an expert at hunting and fishing and is considered a good warrior, and able to comfortably support a home, the chiefs of the two bands are notified and a wedding is arranged, with the two chiefs as head men, and it is always the most elaborate of any doings of the tribe."[5] Informants on various reservations are unable to explain what Armstrong might have meant by an "elaborate wedding." They are emphatic in stating that marriage consisted of nothing more than eating together and sharing the fur robes used as bedding.

Father Pierz wrote that mothers and grandmothers generally decided on the choice of a husband for the young woman. The daughter must marry the man of their choice even should the daughter object to him. The consequence, he adds, being that not seldom does one see unhappy marriages and separations. He continued: "Mothers, however, take likes and dislikes of the young couple into consideration. When mothers of both the young man and the young woman have agreed as to the marriage, and the customary presents have been exchanged, the boy's mother leads him accompanied by other members of the family along with many presents, to the lodge of the girl's mother. The presents are given to the bride's mother and she at once distributes them among her own family. The groom's mother then presents her son to the bride's mother and bids him to be industrious, obedient, and well-behaved. After this the groom presents his hand to his bride and they sit down together. This ends the marriage ceremony."*[6] Gilfillan, too, noted that there was no marriage ceremony.[7]

For an entire year the couple stayed with the bride's parents after which time they established their own household.[8] Miss Densmore observed that the couple usually remained at the girl's home for a while, although they might at once go to live in a lodge of their own.[9]

When annuities began to be paid it was advantageous for a man to have several wives, for the annuity for each child and each woman came to him as head of the house. Sometimes the wives were sisters. At times the wives were found to occupy separate lodges, although they often lived in one.[10]

Separations occurred among the Ojibway. A woman could leave her husband and return to her family and he could then do as he pleased.[11] A man might leave his wife and marry another, feeling no responsibilities, whatsoever, toward his deserted wife and children.[12]

It is difficult to say whether the conditions of marital life within the family on the White Earth Reservation were due to the retention of some trait of the old pattern or whether they were merely the result of the loss of a traditional set of standards and the acceptance of none other.

In the one hundred fifty families, common-law marriages, legal marriages, church marriages, divorce and remarriage, and separation and remarriage were found. Common-law marriages occurred within all generations, in all groups of religious affiliations, and in all types of houses. Twenty-two couples of the one hundred fifty surveyed lived in common-law marriage. Nineteen of these lived in tar-paper shacks; two in frame houses and one in a rehabilitation house.

The couples of the older generations, members of the Midē wiwin, who have lived happily in common-law marriages for years and who are in good faith, should hardly be disturbed in their peaceful lives. Interference from legal authority forcing them to have marriage ceremonies performed according to the socially accepted standards of the citizens of the state of Minnesota would seem unfair. It was difficult, however, to understand how the authorities of three counties in which the reservation is located could be satisfied that they were fulfilling an accepted duty when they permitted common-law marriages among the third generation or among the second generation whose partners mere-

*Translated from the German by the writer.

ly separated to live in public concubinage with another partner. Often this was done with little or no responsibility toward the children of the first marriage.

The couples of the third generation living in common-law marriage in no case pleaded ignorance of the state laws regarding marriage. In several cases they had gotten marriage licenses, but had not exchanged marriage vows. In some cases they had intended to do so after they had lived together a year. "But we couldn't get along that first year, and never have since; so what's the use of tying yourself to a man you can't get along with!" said one woman. In the meantime she intended to live with him "because he supports our kids and I cook for them." Others had been definitely advised by their Catholic parents or Grand Medicine grandparents not to exchange their marriage vows in a Catholic church. "Try it out for one year and if you get along all right, have a church wedding." The Catholic people seemed to be fully aware of the fact that a Catholic may not remarry after a divorce or separation, unless the partner dies.

All parents interviewed were asked: "Why are there so many common-law marriages on the White Earth Reservation?" From answers one might infer the causes involved. One of the factors was probably tradition. One young mother replied: "Living together for one year is an old Indian way, for it was always that way formerly. My old grandmother says that in the old days a couple lived together in the girl's home for a year, and if she and her man got along together they went out and lived by themselves." A seventy-eight-year-old woman who had been married successively to three husbands in common-law marriage said, "Long ago, Indians married that way; they didn't know any better. And I think it is a good way for the young to do today. Let them live together one year and try it out. It will give them a chance to become acquainted with each other."

A young woman, a member of the Midē wiwin, remarked that she thought common-law marriage was an acceptable form for all Indians to live, provided they stayed with their partners. A forty-five-year-old man, father of a family of eight children, did not approve of common-law marriages, but added, "It's always been that way; and today even some that are educated live that way." Another said, "It's Indian style. Before Indians got mixed up with whites they all married that way." One young married man, a member of the Fox tribe, noted that he had never given the matter much thought; he himself had been married in the church. "It's the same way among the Fox and other tribes that I've lived with."

A sixty-eight-year-old woman, who was married to her seventy-one-year-old husband in church in 1937 after living with him seventeen years in common-law marriage, approved of it. She related that recently a fifty-year-old man, father of ten full-grown children, came to live with her "old man's" thirty-five-year-old daughter and that she had no fault to find with them. One of the outstanding Indians on the reservation said, "Young people think nothing about it since they see so many doing it, and it's old Indian way."

Old people, moreover, advise the younger to live common-law marriages. A fifty-year-old woman, mother of four daughters, the oldest of whom was twenty, thought that there were two reasons for common-law marriages: First it was the Indian way of marrying; secondly, many parents advised a daughter to live in common-law marriage so that she might be able to leave her husband in the event that she discovered him to be an unsuitable partner. "My in-laws want all their children and grandchildren to live in common-law marriage for one year. If they don't quarrel during that year, then they want them to be married in their church. My husband and I quarreled, like all couples do the first year of their married life, and my grandmother used to say, 'There you are! That's why I didn't want you to get married in church for a year!'" A woman, forty-nine years of age, and her husband, fifty-five, agreed that it was the "old timers" that wanted it so, and who taught it. "There's a girl twenty years old right out here living with a man fifty. Her mother doesn't want her to get married to him in the church for then she can't leave him anymore. Her mother hopes that some day she will leave him and again receive the Sacraments."

Some Indians thought common-law marriages were occurring because of the lack of law enforcement. "The Indians do it because they can get away with it. There's no law enforcement here." An outstanding Indian in one of the communities said with a good deal of emphasis, "It's a disgrace to our tribe. Times are modern now and all young Indians have gone to school. The law should be enforced!"

Another factor seemed to be the desire to provide a home for themselves and support for their children. Some women whose husbands had deserted them had accepted men who moved in to stay with them. "My children were all small when my man left us, and I had a hard time feeding them. This man is good to my children." A fine old lady of Grand Medicine belief thought the children were better cared for if people who couldn't get along separated and the mother found another partner. "Anyway, that's old Indian style," she added with emphasis. A twenty-four-year-old father said, "People marry that way so they can marry again and have a place to stay in case they are chased out of their home."

Several informants felt that the disapproval of parents to marriages of their children forced some young people to leave home and "to set up housekeeping of their own."

As noted before, it is difficult to know why common-law marriages occur. They may be due to tradition or to pressure of parents. Knowledge that common-law marriage is an accepted form in the community and therefore has little stigma attached to it may also be a cause. It may be due to the lack of a period of company keeping in which couples can learn to know each other. Parenthetically, it may be stated that, should company keeping become part of their social pattern, one wonders where young couples could meet. One- or two-room homes hardly allow for it; recreational places are largely disreputable beer parlors; automobiles, parked on roadsides, provide dangerous privacy and propinquity.

It appeared to the writer, however, that the marriage pattern, so calmly accepted by the Chippewa on the reservation but so annoying and confusing to those out of the group, rested in the traditional culture pattern. It was a curious fact that young couples so married usually lived with the parents of the girl for one year, thereby following a traditional custom.

The following table gives the facts related to marriage as revealed by the study.

TABLE VII

Marriage among One Hundred Fifty Chippewa Indian Families
on the White Earth Reservation in 1938

MARRIAGES	SEVENTY-ONE TAR-PAPER SHACK FAMILIES	SEVENTY-ONE FRAME-HOUSE FAMILIES	EIGHT U.S. REHABILITATION-HOUSE FAMILIES	ALL CASES
Common-law marriages	19	2	1	22
Legal marriages	15	16	2	33
Marriages in Protestant churches	11	6	2	19
Marriages in the Catholic church	26	47	3	76
Total	71	71	8	150
Mixed marriages Midē wiwin and Catholic	3	–	–	3

TABLE VII *(continued)*

MARRIAGES	SEVENTY-ONE TAR-PAPER SHACK FAMILIES	SEVENTY-ONE FRAME-HOUSE FAMILIES	EIGHT U.S. REHABILITATION-HOUSE FAMILIES	ALL CASES
Midē wiwin and Protestant	3	–	–	3
Catholic and Protestant	16	11	–	27
Total	22	11	–	33

CONCLUSIONS

Common-law marriages seemed definitely related to tar-paper shacks. Legal marriages showed no relationship. A larger number of couples of Catholic marriages lived in frame houses than in tar-paper shacks, and the reverse was true of Protestants. A larger number of couples of mixed marriages between Catholics and Protestants lived in tar-paper shacks than in frame houses; all of the mixed marriages between Midē wiwin members and either Catholic or Protestants lived in tar-paper shacks.

ANCESTRY OF PARENTS

Twenty-seven of the parents in the one hundred fifty families were of non-Chippewa descent, but were married to Chippewa. Three of the men were Sioux, Fox, or Cree. Nine of the men of European descent, married to Chippewa women, were of Canadian-French, German, Scandinavian, or Dutch parentage. The fifteen mothers of European descent, married to Chippewa men, were Canadian-French, German, Scandinavian, and Bohemian. Families of European ancestry who lived on the White Earth Reservation and in the surrounding area were large-ly French-Canadians, Germans, Scandinavians, Bohemians, and Finnlanders. It is interesting to note that none had inter-married with Finnlanders although there is a considerable number of them scattered through the reservation.

The three Indian fathers of other tribes lived in tar-paper shacks; so did four of the nine white fathers. Only four of the fifteen white women, however, lived in tar-paper shacks. One might infer from these facts that white women married to Chippewa men are more apt to live in frame houses than are Indian women married to white men.

Gossip had it that some Indian women preferred white husbands since white men supported them better than did Indian men. Another reason was that their children, being less dark, had better opportunities in white communities. White men are suspected of marrying Indian women for the sake of annuities, those for wives and children making a neat sum. Why white women marry Indian men was not known; some thought it must be solely for love!

SEPARATION AND DIVORCE

As may be recalled, separations were allowed by the traditional code of the Chippewa. Formal divorces, however, were unknown to them, probably because there was no legal marriage or because the Chippewa, in their traditional setting, were decidedly individualistic. Most matters were one's own affairs; public opinion, not formal laws, ruled the group.

Eighteen parents in the one hundred fifty families had left their partners, seven of them being legally divorced and the remaining eleven having merely separated. All were remarried, the separated ones merely living in common-law marriages. Tar-paper shacks were housing two legally divorced persons and seven separated ones; frame houses, five divorced persons and three separated ones; rehabilitation houses, one separated woman.

CONCLUSIONS

From the above facts one might infer that frame-house people sought divorces and remarried, while tar-paper shack people merely parted and entered into common-law marriages.

PREVIOUS MARRIAGES

When death takes an Indian parent, the widowed partner, if there is a family, has little choice but to remarry. Grandparents or other relatives may house the family for a while, but houses are too small, as a rule, to shelter two families.

In one hundred twenty-seven of the one hundred fifty homes both parents were living; in twenty-two there was a widowed parent; in one, an unmarried mother and her family of three illegitimate children.

The following are the data on previous marriages as found in the study.

TABLE VIII

Previous Marriages of Parents in One Hundred Fifty Chippewa Indian Families on the White Earth Reservation of Minnesota in 1938

PREVIOUS MARRIAGES	SEVENTY-ONE TAR-PAPER SHACK FAMILIES	SEVENTY-ONE FRAME-HOUSE FAMILIES	EIGHT U.S REHABILITATION-HOUSE FAMILIES	ALL TYPES
Father				
One previous marriage	15	7	–	22
Two previous marriages	3	2	1	6
Three previous marriages	2	1	–	3
Total	20	10	1	31
Mother				
One previous marriage	13	14	1	28
Two previous marriages	1	–	–	1
Three previous marriages	2	–	–	2
Total	16	14	1	31

CONCLUSIONS

Previous marriages showed little relationship to housing as far as the mother was concerned. For fathers, however, they did, for twenty of the tar-paper shack men had been previously married, while only ten of those in the frame houses had.

Of the widowed group, ten widows and one widower lived in tar-paper shacks; eight widows and two widowers in frame houses; one widow in a rehabilitation house. The type of house and being widowed, therefore, showed no significant relationship.

THE AGE OF PARENTS

Traditionally, as noted before, the wife at her first marriage would in all probability be several years younger than her husband. She was of marriageable age at fourteen or fifteen; he only after his first successful hunt, which occurred probably when he was in his twenties. No ethnological material is at hand relative to customs of age requirements for successive marriages in either the literature or in the writer's field notes. From facts gathered in this study one might infer, however, that expediency is a factor.

Most first marriages of the third generation showed nearly the same age for both parents. But unusual variation occurred in the second and third marriages for all groups. Of the tar-paper shack group, thirteen husbands were ten or more years older than their wives, three of them being more than twenty years older. An equal number of wives, namely thirteen, were older than their husbands, five of them being more than five years older.

Of the frame-house group, ten of the husbands exceeded their wives by ten or more years, one of them being more than twenty years older. Eighteen of the wives were five or more years older than their husbands, eight being more than ten years older. Of the entire group two wives were in their teens, one being eighteen and the other nineteen; the youngest husband was twenty-four.

CONCLUSIONS

Unusual variations in the ages of parents appeared to have no relationship to housing, for twenty-six of the cases occurred in tar-paper shacks, and twenty-eight in frame houses. In rehabilitation houses, all wives were younger than their husbands.

FAMILY COMPOSITION AND THE CHILDREN IN THE HOMES

THE AVERAGE FAMILY

The normal Chippewa family in traditional days consisted of father, mother, pre-adolescent sons and daughters, daughters in their early adolescence, and sons not yet of marriageable age. However, other persons were usually members of the household. Possibly, a daughter and her husband in their first year of marriage might be found there. Occasionally one might have found there, too, the mother's disabled parents—although old people were usually expected to care for themselves—or the mother's widowed brother, still in his first year of mourning, and some of his children. If the parents' own children were grown up, they would, without doubt, take a grandchild or two into the home. It was unusual for grandparents not to have adopted one or two children, one of these customarily being a girl. Children were merely declared adopted by the grandparents and were considered so by the group, if the parents raised no objections. There were no adoption ceremonials nor were there legal adoptions. Grandparents reared these children and in turn expected to be, and usually were, cared for by them in their old age.

The Chippewa family of today has changed little from the traditional one. Adult persons are taken in as members, and so are children. This is true of families living in tar-paper shacks as well as of those living in frame houses.

The mean size of families in the two groups differed little. For families living in tar-paper shacks, the mean number of children was 3.79; the mean for all persons, 5.83. The mean number of children for the frame houses was 3.43; that for all persons, 5.47. The mean number of children for the rehabilitation houses was 3.2; that for all persons, 4.2.

THE CHILDREN IN THE FAMILY

In the following table all children ranging from infancy to six years of age are classed as preschool children; all children below eighteen years of age, as children of school age. Several children who had been adopted, or who were considered as part of the family and were treated as such, are included in the groups.

TABLE IX

Children below Eighteen Years of Age in One Hundred Fifty
Chippewa Indian Families on the White Earth Reservation in 1938

PRESCHOOL AND SCHOOL CHILDREN	TAR-PAPER SHACK FAMILIES	FRAME-HOUSE FAMILIES	U.S. REHABILITATION - HOUSE FAMILIES	TOTAL
	Per cent	Per cent	Per cent	Per cent
Preschool children	51	44	5	100
School children	49	46	5	100
Percentage of all children	50	45	5	100

CONCLUSIONS

The above figures indicate that there was little relationship between housing and the number of preschool and school children.

CHILDREN IN BOARDING SCHOOLS

Forty-six of the children in the one hundred fifty families attended resident boarding schools for Indians in 1937–1938. Eighteen of these attended the Catholic mission schools at White Earth and Red Lake; the remaining twenty-eight were in U.S. Government boarding schools at Haskell, Flandreau, Pipestone and Wahpeton. Twenty-eight of the forty-six (sixty per cent) lived in tar-paper shacks, while only eighteen (forty per cent) lived in frame houses. None of the children in rehabilitation houses attended a boarding school since all lived within walking distance of the White Earth district school.

CONCLUSIONS

Attendance of children at boarding school was definitely related to housing, the ratio being two to three in favor of tar-paper shacks. Reasons were: First, overcrowding in the home, for, as noted before, thirty-seven of the tar-paper shacks were one-room homes; secondly, location in isolated places, long distances from school buildings or from school bus service–homes in isolated places usually being tar-paper shacks.

CARE OF HOMELESS CHILDREN

Homeless children on the White Earth Reservation were often cared for in homes of relatives but rarely with the assistance of aid-to-dependent-children funds. Aid is administered only in homes that are considered adequate; very few of the Indian homes were so classified. Because of this condition, homeless children were sometimes placed in one of the boarding schools for Indian children.

Many of them, however, were found in private homes. In the one hundred fifty families, sixty-two mothers were sheltering grandchildren of either legitimate or illegitimate birth while two were housing a niece. The following table summarizes the findings regarding the care of homeless children.

TABLE X

The Care of Homeless Children in One Hundred Fifty
Chippewa Indian Families on the White Earth Reservation in 1938

HOMELESS CHILDREN	SEVENTY-ONE TAR-PAPER SHACK FAMILIES	SEVENTY-ONE FRAME-HOUSE FAMILIES	EIGHT U.S. REHABILITATION-HOUSE FAMILIES	ALL CASES
Care of homeless children				
Homes sheltering children, non-members of family	25	34	5	64
Number of children of legitimate birth				
Both parents dead	16	13	1	30
One parent dead	3	7	–	10

TABLE X *(continued)*

HOMELESS CHILDREN	SEVENTY-ONE TAR-PAPER SHACK FAMILIES	SEVENTY-ONE FRAME-HOUSE FAMILIES	EIGHT U.S. REHABILITATION- HOUSE FAMILIES	ALL CASES
Number of children born out of wedlock	7	22	9	38
Total	26	42	10	78

CONCLUSIONS

Again the difference between the two groups was not significant enough that one might have inferred that sheltering grandchildren as such was related to housing. When the items were broken down, however, we found that twenty-two children born out of wedlock lived in frame houses, while only seven lived in tar-paper shacks.

RETENTION OF THE CHIPPEWA LANGUAGE

Chippewa was spoken by persons of all ages on the reservation. It was the only language spoken, however, by twenty-two or eight per cent of the parents in the one hundred fifty families, fourteen of these living in tar-paper shacks and eight in frame houses. Of the ones living in tar-paper shacks, six were men and eight were women; of the frame-house dwellers, two were men and six were women. It was the only language that preschool children understood in a few of the homes, especially if they were living in the homes of aged grandparents. One such child, a thirteen-year-old girl enrolled at St. Benedict's Mission School for Girls at White Earth in the fall of 1938, was unable to carry on a conversation in English. She invariably sought a playmate who spoke both Chippewa and English to interpret for her.

One hundred fifty-seven or fifty-six per cent of the parents spoke Chippewa fluently. Fifty-four per cent of these lived in tar-paper shacks, forty-one per cent in frame houses, and five in rehabilitation houses. Nineteen others (seven in tar-paper shacks and twelve in frame houses) understood Chippewa well, but did not speak it.

CONCLUSIONS

A larger number of tar-paper shack people, therefore, had an acquaint-
ance with the Chippewa language than did frame-house dwellers.

EDUCATIONAL OPPORTUNITIES OF PARENTS

FORMAL EDUCATION

The early Chippewa had no formal schooling such as we know it–
schooling given by professional teachers in school buildings–but they
did receive instructions from their elders in ethical standards, moral
code, and vocational guidance and practice.

They were taught the ethical standards of their people around the
campfires of the wigwam through the long winter evenings. These
lessons were usually embodied in stories. Copway tells of the lessons of
his own childhood:

> Some of these stories are most exciting, and so intensely interesting, that
> I have seen children during their relation, whose tears would flow quite
> plentifully, and their breasts heave with thoughts too big for utterance.
>
> Night after night for weeks have I sat and eagerly listened to these sto-
> ries. The days following, the characters would haunt me at every step, and
> every moving leaf would seem to be a voice of a spirit. To those days I
> look back with pleasurable emotions. . . . [13]

The moral code was taught to boys and girls at the age of puberty,
usually by the grandparents or, in their absence, by elders living in the
community. A change of voice in the boy gave notice that he had
reached puberty and that he was to be instructed in the duties and obligations of manhood. His father or grandfather instructed him in the
powers he was expected to receive while fasting in a lonely place, resting
on a platform or in a "nest" up in a tree, "where the large branches
begin." Here the boy fasted from four to ten days and dreamed. His
father or some older man visited the place daily and brought him a little
food and some water, and instructed him "in all things that were expected of him as a man."

The girl, too, received instructions at puberty. She was isolated, but
not far from home, at first menstruation, in a small circular wigwam built
by herself with the aid of her mother or grandmother. Here she lived
from four to ten days, receiving daily instructions in motherhood, its
duties and obligations. (While discussing the problem of the unmarried
mother included in this study, two mothers, one in a frame house and
one in a tar-paper shack, volunteered the information that they "made
the girls stay upstairs, away from everybody" at puberty, and that they

had asked the grandmothers of the girls to instruct them in motherhood during the days of isolation. "My girls have certainly settled down since then and don't do any more running around!" said one mother.)

After puberty rites, boys and girls were no longer considered children; they had outgrown the first stage of Chippewa life, namely childhood, and had entered the second, that of "old man" and "old woman." They were ready now to begin their vocational training.

Parents instructed them in the work expected of them as adults, and insisted that they learn by helping them at all times. Boys went on hunting expeditions, and, at times, on the war path with the father and older men. Boys, too, learnt to construct bows and arrows and canoes.

The girl learnt all the household duties, such as gathering and chopping wood, making maple sugar, gathering wild rice, preparing and cooking food, sewing, making wigwams, mats, and birch-bark vessels and beadwork. Some of the old women told how they stole away from work, whenever an opportunity presented itself, to play with their dolls, only to be laughed at or chided by the older women. Back to work they must go, doing things on a small scale first, and eventually receiving praise and recognition from elders for a piece of work begun and completed by their own personal efforts—efforts which might have resulted in a tanned hide, a pair of moccasins, a wigwam, or some maple sugar.

Most persons of the first generation on the reservation, the ones whose youth was largely spent in the old culture, received little formal education of the American type. Most of the second generation had opportunities for doing so in boarding schools, but only a few of them were interested enough to attend several years. All of the present generation have had opportunities either at boarding or day schools. The present generation, too, has had opportunities for high-school or vocational education in schools on or off the reservation.

The following table presents the findings regarding the formal education of the parents in the families. Some homes had been deprived of a parent by death or desertion, hence there were only 279 parents in the one hundred fifty families.

TABLE XI

Parents and Their Formal Education in One Hundred Fifty
Chippewa Indian Families on the White Earth Reservation in 1938

PARENTS AND FORMAL EDUCATION	SEVENTY-ONE TAR-PAPER SHACK FAMILIES	SEVENTY-ONE FRAME-HOUSE FAMILIES	EIGHT U.S. REHABILITATION-HOUSE FAMILIES	ALL TYPES
Parents in the homes				
Fathers	61	66	6	133
Mothers	70	68	8	146
Total	131	134	14	279
Formal education of parents				
Illiterate				
Fathers	19	13	–	32
Mothers	18	9	–	27
Total	37	22	–	59
Attended grades between first and eighth				
Fathers	25	26	2	53
Mothers	26	25	2	53
Total	51	51	4	106
Entered eighth grade				
Fathers	9	14	3	26
Mothers	17	15	4	36
Total	26	29	7	62
Spent some time in high school				
Fathers	3	12	1	16
Mothers	14	20	2	36
Total	17	32	3	52
Grand total	131	134	14	279

One of the men and six of the women entered the twelfth grade, but only three women completed the high school course. One of these three lived in a tar-paper shack and two were living in frame houses. Of those who had learnt a trade or had had professional training, one, a blacksmith, lived in a tar-paper shack; while a carpenter, a business woman, and a teacher lived in frame houses.

The mode for formal education for both men and women in tar-paper shacks occurred at the sixth grade. The mode for men in frame houses occurred at the fifth grade; that for women, at the seventh.

CONCLUSIONS

There appeared to be a definite relationship between housing and formal education of parents. The number of illiterate parents living in tar-paper shacks exceeded that of the frame-house group by fourteen per cent, while the number of frame-house parents who spent some time in high school exceeded that of the tar-paper shack group, who availed themselves of the same opportunity, by thirty per cent.

EDUCATIONAL OPPORTUNITIES IN BOARDING SCHOOLS

Boarding-school opportunities had been offered to the parents in various localities and under two supervisions, namely those of the U.S. Government schools and of the Catholic mission schools. Government schools were located at Haskell, Kansas; Carlisle, Pennsylvania; Genoa, Nebraska; Flandreau, South Dakota; Wahpeton, North Dakota; Pipestone, Minnesota; Morris, Minnesota; and Odanah, Wisconsin; on the White Earth Reservation at the White Earth Boarding School, at Bealieu, and at Pine Point. The mission schools were located on the Red Lake and the White Earth reservations, at St. Joseph, and at St. John's, all of them in Minnesota. Both government and mission schools were open to all Indian children, tuition being paid from tribal funds. One wonders why twenty-one per cent on the reservation should be illiterate when such fine opportunities for education had been offered them. One has to bear in mind, however, that many of the parents were of school age before the days of swift transportation, and that giving their children an educational opportunity in a boarding school meant long months of severance from them.

Had no other factors entered into educational opportunities than attendance at a boarding school, one might say boarding-school education and housing were not related. For of the two hundred seventy-nine parents, seventy-nine per cent attended one or several of the above-named schools. Forty-six per cent of these lived in tar-paper shacks at the time of this study. Forty-nine per cent lived in frame houses. All the mothers, eight in number, and five of the six fathers living in rehabilitation houses had attended a boarding school. Nor did length of attendance enter as a factor, for some who attended but one year and others who attended from five to eight lived in both types of houses.

Neither was attendance at a type of school a factor, if the total number of the parents is taken into consideration. The largest number, thirty-nine, attended the White Earth Boarding School, a U.S. Government school. Of these twenty-two (eleven men and eleven women) lived in tar-paper shacks; seventeen (fifteen men and two women) in frame houses. Of the thirty women who attended St. Benedict's Mission School for Girls, also located at White Earth, fourteen lived in tar-paper shacks and sixteen in frame houses. Three of the eight women living in rehabilitation houses attended St. Benedict's Mission School, while two of the men attended the White Earth Boarding School.

Nor did attendance at Carlisle–a school whose students are outstanding in leadership, intelligence, and knowledge, and who are easily distinguishable in any Indian group–show its effects in the choice of a house. Five Carlisle students, two men and three women, lived in tar-paper shacks, while only two women lived in frame houses. The remaining schools who had a larger number of pupils living in tar-paper shacks were Haskell, Red Lake, and Wahpeton. Those having a larger number living in frame houses were Morris, Flandreau, Beaulieu, St. John's, Genoa, Pine Point, and St. Joseph. Pipestone had an equal number in each type of house.

To the question: "Why did you not continue your education?" the men invariably answered, "I was not interested." They were not interested in the type of education that was being given them; neither in the formal education nor in the farming and the dairying which were taught at most of the schools.

The women were interested, but many returned home because either they were lonesome for home or their parents were lonesome for them. "Mother walked over one hundred miles from here to St. Joe and took my sister and me home. School had just started, and it was the first time we were away from home. We walked back home; she packed my little sister on her back most of the way."

In answer to the question: "Is there anything you now wish you had learnt at boarding school?" the women invariably said that they wished they had learnt to sew. "I can stitch fine; but I can't cut a dress nor can I make old clothes over well. I'm learning it now in our Homemakers' Club, and it helps a lot in keeping the kids dressed." When one recalls that most of these families live on a subsistence standard, the ability for mothers to remodel discarded clothes, such as are received from friends or gotten at salvage sales, is of very real importance.

The men felt the need of knowing a trade. "Some of the W.P.A. jobs call for knowledge of a trade and those who have that knowledge get good pay," said one man. Another, "My job at school was to milk cows and keep their beds clean. I used to get good praise for doing that, but no W.P.A. jobs call for that type of skill! And anyway, it wouldn't pay to do that now, for farmers can't pay as much as W.P.A. jobs."

CONCLUSIONS

Significant findings related to formal education are probably these: First, women exceeded men by thirty-four in boarding-school attendance; by eighteen in eighth-grade attendance; by five in twelfth-grade attendance; and by three in the completion of high school—none of the men completing the twelfth grade. Secondly, housing and attendance at boarding school are not related.

EXPERIENCE OFF THE RESERVATION

It was thought that possibly some experience off the reservation, some travel or mingling with white people affected housing and living conditions. With this in mind, the birthplace of each parent was included in the study, as well as any experience by contacts in travel to places off the reservation or in visits to the two largest cities in Minnesota, namely St. Paul and Minneapolis. Information regarding trips to states bounding Minnesota and to travel to any other parts of this continent or the world was also included.

The study revealed that of the one hundred fifty families, sixty per cent of the parents were born on the White Earth Reservation; eighteen per cent, on other reservations—mostly Chippewa reservations; and twenty-two per cent, in white communities.

The study further revealed that thirty-three per cent of the parents had never been much farther than one hundred miles in any direction beyond the reservation. Objectives of trips were usually berry picking, sugar making, wild-rice gathering, medical attention, or visiting relatives or friends.

Sixty-four per cent of the parents had not been in either St. Paul or Minneapolis.

Some of the parents had made trips into states bounding Minnesota. Of the tar-paper shack dwellers one had been in Canada, eight in Wisconsin, six in Iowa, twenty in South Dakota, and forty-one in North Dakota. Of the frame-house occupants five had been in Canada, nineteen in Wisconsin, eleven in Iowa, thirty-four in South Dakota, and forty-nine in North Dakota. The following table indicates the experience of the parents off the reservation.

80 CHIPPEWA FAMILIES

TABLE XII

Experience Off the Reservation of the Parents of One Hundred Fifty
Chippewa Indian Families on the White Earth Reservation in 1938

EXPERIENCE OFF THE RESERVATION	TAR-PAPER SHACK FAMILIES	FRAME-HOUSE FAMILIES	U.S. REHABILITATION-HOUSE FAMILIES	NO. OF PARENTS
Birthplace of parents				
Father				
White Earth Reservation	42	47	5	94
Other Chippewa reservation	6	5	1	12
In white community	13	14	–	27
Total	61	66	6	133
Mother				
White Earth Reservation	44	45	8	97
Other Chippewa reservation	13	6	–	19
In white community	13	17	–	30
Total	70	68	8	146
Grand total	131	134	14	279
Experience off the reservation				
Travelled less than 100 miles off reservation				
Fathers	18	7	2	27
Mothers	35	27	3	65
Total	53	34	5	92
Never visited St. Paul or Minneapolis				
Fathers	43	35	2	80
Mothers	52	45	5	102
Total	95	80	7	182
Trip into states bounding Minnesota				
Fathers	34	69	6	109
Mothers	42	49	4	95
Total	76	118	10	204
World War service abroad				
Fathers	1	4	–	5
Member of Indian baseball team				
Fathers	–	3	–	3

Eleven of the frame-house people had been to one or several of the following states: Montana, Illinois, District of Columbia, and Michigan. Nine of the tar-paper shack people had been in either Montana, Missouri, or Illinois. One tar-paper shack man had been to the South and to Cuba.

The three frame-house men who had belonged to Indian baseball teams had spent some time in many of the states—one having been in all but six and another in all but Rhode Island.

CONCLUSIONS

Place of birth and residence in either a tar-paper shack or frame house were barely related, for of the sixty per cent born on the White Earth Reservation, thirty-three per cent lived in tar-paper shacks and twenty-seven per cent in frame houses; of the twenty-two per cent born in white communities, ten per cent lived in tar-paper shacks and twelve per cent in frame houses. Experience off the reservation and travel, however, seemed related to housing. The number of tar-paper shack persons that had never been far beyond the reservation exceeded the frame-house group by twenty-one per cent; those who had not been to St. Paul or Minneapolis, by eight per cent. Furthermore, more persons in frame houses had had opportunities for extended trips and experience in white communities than had those living in tar-paper shacks.

RELIGIOUS AFFILIATIONS OF PARENTS

THE MIDĒ WIWIN OR GRAND MEDICINE SOCIETY

The Midē wiwin, the Society of the Midē or Shamans—popularly designated as the Grand Medicine Society—is the custodian of the traditional religion of the Chippewa. Warren defined it as the Chippewa "mode of worshipping the Great Spirit, and securing life in this and a future world, and of conciliating the lesser spirits, who in their belief, people earth, sky, and waters . . ."[14]

The Midē wiwin consists of an indefinite number of Midē of both sexes. There are four separate and distinct degrees in the society, namely those of the weasel, the owl, the hawk, and the eagle. Each degree has its own songs and its own designs of face painting. Each advanced degree, too, has greater power or stronger "medicine" than the preceding one. "Medicine," or "Grand Medicine," a term used to designate knowledge of remedies for illness, powers of prediction, or abilities of penetration into past events, is always secret information. Grand Medicine is feared and respected by non-members, and is usually asso-

ciated with the contents of a "medicine bag." One such bag came under
the writer's observation among the Menomenee of Wisconsin, also a
Woodland Algonquian tribe. It contained two eagle feathers, a red ten-
nis ball, and some smoking tobacco.

The Midē wiwin holds an annual ceremony, popularly called the
Grand Medicine Dance, usually in the spring at which time new members are admitted. Members speak of themselves as belonging to the
society of the particular group that accepted them, designating names
usually being those of a band or village. "My old woman and I both
belong to the Leech Lake Midē wiwin; our neighbors here belong to the
Ponemah one." Celebrations require four days and consist primarily of
dancing and singing to the rhythm of the Midē wiwin drums and rattles,
of offerings made by candidates, of ceremonial smoking, and of sacrifices
of four dogs. All members participate. The ceremonial is conducted in
the Midē lodge, a framework of saplings covered with boughs and
resembling an elongated wigwam.

The Midē wiwin still exists on the White Earth Reservation.
Membership of persons in the one hundred fifty families included persons of all generations, ranging in age from four years to 102. Grand
Medicine Dances are held every spring at Ponsford and at Elbow Lake.
Members belonging to lodges, other than those of Ponsford and Elbow
Lake, travel many miles in the spring time to be present at the ceremonial of their own group. Several had made a round trip of four hundred
miles in the spring of 1938 to do so. After reading Hoffman's description
of the Midē wiwin one is led to believe, however, that the ceremonials
on the White Earth Reservation are losing much of their earlier interest
and exactness.[15] The Ponsford group adopted two children, "Just old
enough to know what was going on," in June, 1938. The participating
members did carry out the dancing to the rhythm of the drum and rattle. They sang the songs, smoked, and killed the dogs. The mothers of
the two children offered gifts of clothing, rag-braided rugs, yards of calico, and tin and galvanized pails. But their faces were unpainted, and
their Midē lodge was an uncovered framework of saplings with only a
row of cedar twigs fastened to it for about the depth of a foot, close to
the ground. On the Lac Courte Orielle and the Red Lake reservations,
Grand Medicine Dances drew large crowds of non-participants. It was
not so at Ponsford; only eleven adults, ten women and one man, were
participant observers. The larger number of the visiting people were not
interested. They were for the most part non-members who had come
merely because they had transported their aged relatives who were
members. One group of men was listening to a radio announcement of

a baseball game in one of the homes, while another was visiting in the shade of the house. Children played noisily about the place.

It is a curious fact, too, that of the four families now living on the plot of ground on which the ceremonial was held—the traditional place for the Midē wiwin ceremonial at Ponsford and the place in which the framework of the Midē lodge remains from year to year—only one man was a member, and he was living in common-law marriage with a Catholic woman who had left her husband. Two of the four families were practicing Catholics, while the third was an Episcopal.

CONCLUSIONS

Of the parents in the one hundred fifty families, thirteen (4.7 per cent), six men and seven women, were members of the Midē wiwin. All of these lived in tar-paper shacks.

CHRISTIAN CHURCH AFFILIATIONS

Christian churches that have adherents on the White Earth Reservation are the Catholic, the Episcopal, the Methodist and the Gospel Alliance. Information regarding church affiliations for the parents of the families of this study were recorded as given by them. Subsequent checking with pastors or with reliable and practicing members of the churches revealed that only approximately one-third of the members, however, attended Sunday services. The following table is based on information received from the parents. Of the Protestant parents three were Methodist; two, Gospel Alliance; and the remainder, Episcopal. Sixty-six per cent of the parents were Catholic.

TABLE XIII

Religious Affiliation of Parents of One Hundred Fifty
Chippewa Indian Families on the White Earth Reservation in 1938

RELIGIOUS AFFILIATION	SEVENTY-ONE TAR-PAPER SHACK FAMILIES	SEVENTY-ONE FRAME-HOUSE FAMILIES	EIGHT U.S. REHABILITATION-HOUSE FAMILIES
	Per cent	Per cent	Per cent
Midē wiwin	10	–	–
Catholic	54	82	60
Protestant	36	18	40
Total	100	100	100

CONCLUSIONS

All of the Grand Medicine adherents lived in tar-paper shacks. Twice as many Protestants lived in tar-paper shacks as in frame houses, while the number of Catholics living in frame houses was to the number in tar-paper shacks, approximately as eight is to five.

POLITICAL EXPRESSIONS OF PARENTS

TRADITIONAL POLITICS

The traditional political unit among the Chippewa was the band. Each band, or village, was headed by a chief who was assisted–or in his absence replaced by–one of the subchiefs. Both chiefs and subchiefs inherited their posts.[16] Bands consisted of families numbering from five to fifty or more. All persons of a band past puberty composed the tribal council, the tribal council being the advisory body of the chief.

The principal duties of the chief consisted of presiding at the councils of his bands, of making decisions that affected the general welfare, and of settling small disputes. He also represented his band at the payment of annuities, at the signing of treaties, and at large gatherings of his tribe.

All bands of the entire tribe considered themselves affiliated with one of two main groups of Chippewa, namely with either the Mississippi Bands or the Lake Superior Bands. The chiefs of all the bands of one group, or at times the chiefs of all bands of both groups, met in council convened for the purpose of discussing matters of general importance, such as deciding on war or peace, on the sale of land, or on treaties with the United States Government.[17] A chief at such general councils was expected to follow the directions received from his own band before setting out for general meetings. Should anything occur in which he needed advice, he conferred with subchiefs who had accompanied him.

Voting by ballot was unknown to the early Chippewa. They had a right, however, as indicated before, to express their opinions at council meetings. This right extended to both men and women.[18]

Women could, at times, also act as chiefs.

> The head chief of the Pillagers, Flatmouth, has for several years resided in Canada, his sister, Ruth Flatmouth, is in her brother's absence the acknowledged Queen, or leader of the Pillagers; two other women of hereditary right acted as leaders of their respective bands, and at the request of the chiefs were permitted to sign the agreements.[19]

There are no longer any chiefs on the White Earth Reservation. Councils, however, continue to exist, being found in most of the villages on the reservation. As may be recalled, an Indian man or woman of any band who is on the Chippewa roll and has attained the age of twenty-one years is eligible to membership. The Indians say this is their manner of continuing the earlier council meetings. Matters of general interest are expected to be discussed at meetings, and annually delegates for general meetings of the entire tribe are elected, voting being done by ballot.

The ballot, too, is used in the selection of annual delegates to the Tribal Council of the Minnesota Chippewa. In fact, the ballot is now generally used in all matters of tribal interest.

REFERENDUM VOTE FOR JUNE 18, 1938

In a referendum vote calling for choice of location for agency headquarters of the Consolidated Chippewa Agency, held on June 18, 1938, throughout the Consolidated Chippewa Jurisdiction, the ballot was used. The names of several centers at which headquarters might be located were printed on the ballot, while space for any additional choice of the voter was provided for.

One hundred sixty-eight, or sixty per cent, of the parents in the one hundred fifty families cast a vote (only persons of Chippewa descent over twenty-one years of age being allowed to do so). Of the fathers living in tar-paper shacks all but fourteen voted; of the mothers, more than half did not vote. Of those living in frame houses, twelve of the fathers and thirteen of the mothers did not vote. Neither did one of the men and two of the women living in rehabilitation houses.

CONCLUSIONS

The difference between the number of non-voting fathers living in tar-paper shacks and those living in frame houses is not significant; the difference between the mothers, however, is, many more non-voting mothers living in tar-paper shacks than in frame houses. Mothers gave as reasons for non-voting the care of small babies, illness, or the inability to get to the polling stations, their husbands having had opportunities of so doing while coming home from work. Some non-voters were definitely not interested in the location of the headquarters and therefore did not vote.

STATE PRIMARY ELECTIONS OF JUNE 20, 1938

As citizens of Minnesota, all Chippewa voters have the right of franchise in all matters submitted to the voters of the state. One hundred eighty-nine of the parents, or sixty-nine per cent, voted at the state primaries held on June 20, 1938. Sixteen of the men living in tar-paper shacks did not vote; while thirty-two, or nearly half, of the women did not. Most of the non-voters in tar-paper shacks lived in Ponsford. Of parents living in frame houses, fourteen of the men and twenty-six of the women did not vote. None of the Maple Grove and Elbow Lake communities and only half of the White Earth group voted. Non-voters were either not interested in the election or forgot the date. All of those living in rehabilitation houses voted.

It is interesting to note the manner in which non-English speaking Chippewa select their candidates. Men running for office call at the Indian homes and leave their electioneering cards containing name and photographic print of themselves. The non-English speaking Chippewa listen to the discussions about candidates that are being carried on in the Chippewa language among their people and later make their choice according to their judgments. If conversation has not been of an informative kind, they select their candidates by studying the faces on the electioneering cards. One old man remarked, "When I hear a man talk I can tell his character pretty well; but I never make a mistake if I study his face!" When setting out for the polling stations, they take the cards of the candidates for whom they wish to vote with them, and ask the one assisting them in the ballot booth to check the names of those whose cards they have.

CONCLUSIONS

More of the tar-paper shack dwellers than of the frame-house people neglected to vote in the primaries.

SOCIAL PROBLEMS OF THE FAMILIES

THE UNMARRIED MOTHER

The problem of the unmarried mother is one of the greatest on the White Earth Reservation. Law-enforcing groups that deal with White Earth Indians are making little effort of either a preventive or a corrective nature. Their opinion is that it is useless, that the Indian's nature is responsible for his deviation from right, and that there is little that can be done about it. "We expect too much from the present-day Indians. They are only two or three generations removed from their native, primitive, and wild life and continue living it," they say.

The Indian parents, on the other hand, say it is impossible to control the youth of today; that they have learnt the white man's ways in schools and elsewhere, and will not listen to their elders any more.

The writer's ethnological field notes taken on six Chippewa reservations and dealing largely with family life give no indication that there was loose moral living among the Chippewa women in the early day. The writer, too, has searched the literature dealing with this tribe, in vain, to find any reference to it. Armstrong in 1892 gave definite expression to the high moral standards of the Chippewa women, although he notes that the morals were changing, and lays the blame on contact with white men.[20] Most writers do not speak of it, leading one to infer that morals of Chippewa women could not have been so loose as some contemporaries of today would have it.

The following are some of the comments made by the older generation on the White Earth Reservation: "This immoral conduct is a disgrace to our tribe. A stolen child (this being the Chippewa expression for an illegitimate child) was the rarest occurrence in our day," comments one. Another says, "If a man got a girl into trouble when I was young, it wasn't safe for him to stay in the tribe." "In old days, it was a disgrace and a crime for a girl to fall away. It couldn't happen very easily either, for girls stayed close to home then. Today girls, eleven, twelve, thirteen-years old get drunk and sometimes lie along the roadside intoxicated. Any hobo can come up to them and they won't even remember it when they sober up." A full-blooded woman, outstanding in her community, told of having heard, when young, of a girl who gave birth to her "stolen child" in the woods: "It was always said that she had killed the child right after it was born. Everybody in the band used to speak about it. The girl died soon after." Another says, "Men and women married much younger than they do now and there were few illegitimate children. If an Indian man got an Indian girl into trouble and then did not marry her, he was in very bad favor with the tribe. At times he was compelled by the tribe to marry the girl; and if he refused to do so, he was driven from the tribe."

Several factors may have been responsible for high moral living in the early day. It is certain that a girl was of marriageable age as soon after puberty as she was able to do all the work that was expected of a housewife. In the interim, she was seldom out of her mother's sight. In the absence of her mother, some older woman designated by the mother was responsible for the girl. Furthermore, adolescent girls were never permitted to sleep away from home. Nor were a boy and a girl allowed to walk together. "If a man liked a girl, he would go to see her in the presence of her parents, and then only in daytime, never at night."

Conditions have changed radically since early days. One of the old men on the White Earth Reservation remarked that two things were being much talked about at the same time not many years ago. One was the airplane; the other the women who were disgracing the tribe.

It was estimated by some who knew local conditions well, that in White Earth village two girls out of every ten under eighteen years of age have had one or two illegitimate children. There were several women on the reservation who had had four, no two having the same father. Where paternity was known the mother gave the child the father's name; consequently one found four children, who considered themselves siblings, known by four different surnames.

The following table gives the items regarding unmarried mothers as found in the one hundred fifty families:

TABLE XIV

Unmarried Mothers and Their Children in One Hundred Fifty
Chippewa Indian Families on the White Earth Reservation in 1938

UNMARRIED MOTHERS AND THEIR CHILDREN	TAR-PAPER SHACK FAMILIES	FRAME-HOUSE FAMILIES	U.S. REHABILITATION-HOUSE FAMILIES	ALL CASES
Unmarried mothers				
With one child	5	9	–	14
With two children	1	3	2	6
With three children	–	1	1	2
With four children	–	1	–	1
Total	6	14	3	23
Total number of children born out of wedlock	7	22	7	36

More than twice as many unmarried mothers, therefore, lived in frame houses than in tar-paper shacks. It may be recalled that a larger number of families of Catholic-church affiliation lived in frame houses than did Protestants.

Since this study did not include the unmarried mother situation as such, the writer is not prepared to give reliable information as to factors involved in the problem. It is possible, however, that the unmarried mothers of Catholic-church affiliation had been taught the church's teaching that voluntary abortion is murder. As a consequence, it is possible that more children were born to them than to adherents of the Protestant churches, some of which do not agree with this teaching. No attempt was made by the writer to obtain information as to the number and the persons in the families who resorted to abortive methods. Several informants, however, volunteered names of four women on the reservation who possess information on primitive Chippewa methods of abortion, and who dispense its formula.

Other factors in the unmarried mother situation seem to be the breaking down of tribal authority and disciplinary control, the scarcity of proper leisure-time activities, a dearth of wholesome recreation, easy access to liquor, lack of control of public opinion, and the need of law enforcement.

The breaking down of the dominant social order of the old culture has done away with the institutionalized controls of social conduct, and the third generation on the White Earth Reservation is reaping the results. There is no doubt that the native culture has been suppressed by the terrific impact of European civilization. Group control from within is necessary in any civilization, and this control is nearly always exercised by the silent example, as well as by the teachings, of the elders and the respected persons in the group. Such controls were exercised among the primitive Chippewa by the parents and grandparents. Today their control is gone; they feel dejected and discouraged and without resource in the present situation, for they are fully aware that the pattern they know so well does not coincide with that which their children and grandchildren are being taught. "You are now citizens of the United States and no longer Indians. You must live like the white man," the children are told. The old guard is confused; it wonders what in the white man's civilization is worthy of imitation. It feels it has not been able to keep up with the times and hence retires discouraged and heartsick.

In all well-organized groups of life, public opinion and the encouragement of good example are forces for social control. Public opinion on the White Earth Reservation, however, means little to most third-generation persons. Group sanctions, customs, and *mores* of the old culture have little value in their estimation. Furthermore, the standards which they have adopted are tolerated in the group, since "there is nothing else to do about it." The illegitimate child is received into the family of the girl without question and is supported the same as the parents' own children. The force of good example hardly exists as a factor. Drinking and carousing occurs among so large a number of the second generation that parents feel their children may have lost respect for them; in any event, parents say that children do not hesitate to remind them of it.

The laws of Minnesota provide for the establishing of paternity by court action with the subsequent obligation of the father to support his child. Rarely is paternity of an Indian child of illegitimate birth established. County child welfare boards, under whose jurisdiction this duty falls, give as reasons for non-enforcement of the law that the girl is usually not anxious to establish paternity; that she is often promiscuous and does not know who the father of her child is; that conception has taken place in a drunken brawl; or that, in the event paternity is established, the father seldom has money to support the child. And hence, no legal action is any longer being taken.

THE LIQUOR PROBLEM

The Chippewa in their traditional culture had no intoxicating liquor. Smoking, chewing, and drinking decoctions of steeped herbs and roots gave them some exhilaration, but none of these caused loss of judgment, of consciousness, or of control of faculties. Today, intoxication is one of the evils on the White Earth Reservation. It is agreed among respectable whites and Indians alike that persons habitually addicted to drinking on the White Earth Reservation should be defined as those who drink to excess following every, or nearly every pay day–pay days occurring every first and third week of the month. Liquor is sold only on a cash basis, and cash is on hand only when pay checks are on hand. Table XV gives the findings regarding intoxication in the families.

TABLE XV

Drinking to Intoxication in One Hundred Fifty
Chippewa Indian Families on the White Earth Reservation in 1938

DRINKING TO EXCESS	TAR-PAPER SHACK FAMILIES	FRAME-HOUSE FAMILIES	U.S. REHABILITATION-HOUSE FAMILIES	ALL CASES
Both parents	4	4	–	8
Both parents and adolescent youth	1	1	–	2
One parent and adolescent youth	4	2	–	6
Father only	6	9	–	15
Mother only	1	2	–	3
Adolescent youth only	–	2	2	4
Total	16	20	2	38

Although it is unlawful according to a federal statute to sell liquor to an Indian, it is possible in every community on the White Earth Reservation, or on its outskirts, for an Indian to procure intoxicating beverages, namely beer or hard liquor, or both. Indian men, women, and minors, even girls eleven, twelve and thirteen years of age, have access to these places.

A confusing situation seems to exist regarding the enforcement of law and order relative to Indians. In the days of treaties, the Indians were dealt with as distinct political units and considered capable of managing their own affairs. Law enforcement lay within their jurisdiction. Gradually, however, they became wards of the United States Government and were considered incompetent. During this period the Federal Government controlled law and order. Finally, in 1924, Congress declared all Indians born within the limits of the United States to be citizens.[21] As citizens, therefore, Indians are subject today to the law and order of the state and counties in which they reside. The state, however, does not seem to take the matter seriously, for although there is ample machinery for law enforcement in the state of Minnesota, it is evident that little of it is exercised on the White Earth Reservation.

After discussing the factors involved in the liquor problem, with both Indians and whites, it seemed that the law which makes the selling of liquor to an Indian a federal offense should be repealed. The Indians resented it, and the whites thought that the Indian was justified in doing so, since he is a citizen of the country and not a ward or minor under the guardianship of the United States. The law is obsolete in any event. A quarter-blood Indian is on the roll and has therefore the status of an Indian, but he may be indistinguishable from a white man. In places where there is any attempt to enforce the law, smuggling or home-brew results with effects that are worse than those of the saloon. The following is an Indian's account of smuggling: "Indians can't get liquor in any saloon, but it's really not hard to get it. At the present time there are so many hobos who live around in box cars. Well, maybe one of them is dry, and he comes up to an Indian who is also dry and who has a little money. The Indian gives him the money and the hobo buys a little bottle of liquor. He comes back, takes a swallow of it, and gives the rest to the Indian, and soon a couple of Indians are drunk. Sometimes it happens that the hobo accepts the money, takes to the railroad track and away he goes! And the Indian gets nothing!"

A lack of will-power, self-control, and determination on the part of the Indian is the largest factor, no doubt. Indians admit this. In the absence of recreational facilities and leisure-time activities the evening of every pay day is looked forward to by many as an outing, a legitimate relaxation. Another factor is unquestionably the unscrupulous owner of beer parlors and road houses. Profit is his aim; the morals of adults and minors, especially since "they are only Indians," is legitimate prey for his avarice.

Evil results of intoxication on the reservation were several. First of all, human personalities were degraded thereby. Frequently one heard respectable persons on the reservation say, "You wouldn't know so-and-so any longer since he has taken to drink." Secondly, parents drink to the neglect of their children and home. All but a very few of the homes included in the study needed repairing and household equipment. Many families needed clothing, and in many instances, a supplement to their diet. Drinking parents do not seem to realize the value and significance of W.P.A. jobs. Thirdly, the unmarried mother problem appeared to be closely allied to drinking. As noted before, many of the unmarried mothers were unable to identify the father of the child. "I was so drunk, I didn't even know anything had happened," was a frequent comment.

THE PROBLEM OF YOUTH

Adolescent boys and girls on the reservation, without doubt, create social problems, but they themselves, too, have a problem. They are greatly in need of encouragement, advice, and guidance while on the reservation. Those who have ambitions to leave the reservation need a contact person during the time of transition from the reservation into white communities. Once away from the reservation, they need big brothers and big sisters.

Many of those who have had educational opportunities beyond the eighth grade or high school have developed ambitions and desires for a better standard of living, for economic independence, and for sociability other than that which their inadequate homes and environment can provide. One can hardly be in error in saying that there are practically no opportunities on the reservation for the fulfillment of these legitimate ambitions.

Without a larger income, or a wise expenditure of the present income, the family standards cannot be raised. Opportunities on the reservation for earning even a sufficient amount for clothing are rare, consisting of several government jobs for girls and a few N.Y.A. jobs for both boys and girls.

Those who wish to continue their education in vocational training schools or in schools of higher learning need government loans with which to buy clothing and defray expenses. Loans are sometimes delayed because of late or incomplete applications, and for other reasons, leaving the young man or woman in discouragement and bewilderment as to the next step to take.

Once a desire for further study or for betterment of any sort has developed in the youth, there is need for advice and guidance. There is not only the difficulty in the selection of a proper school or place of employment but, in the case of the Indian youth especially if he is dark-skinned, the additional problem of being permitted to enter and, once having received admission, of being understood, especially so if his home environment and training to any extent followed the traditional pattern. The Indian youth is not only struggling with the normal difficulties of growing up, he is also going through a transition from a simple—and in some cases tribal life—to a complex, civilized living. The White Earth Reservation youth need a contact person therefore.

Once a choice of school or place of employment has been made and admission has been received, it is of vital importance that there be some understanding person in the new place of abode in whom the young man or woman finds a substitute for the elders of his own family. He needs to be given a sense of security and affection. He needs guidance in the adjustment to socially accepted ways of whites. It might not be a difficult matter to find some mature man or woman of Chippewa extraction in a number of our large cities—persons who would be interested in guiding and protecting a youth of their own tribe. Names of Chippewa residing in our large cities could easily be gotten from the roll at the headquarters of the Consolidated Chippewa Agency. A fair number of White Earth Chippewa of fine repute and of economic independence are now located in St. Paul and Minneapolis. It is possible that these could be interested in forming a Chippewa big brother and big sister organization.

In the one hundred fifty homes of our study there were sixty-four families with adolescent youths. Twenty-four were living in tar-paper shacks, thirty-eight in frame houses, and two in rehabilitation houses. These young men and women have probably little to look forward to but the rearing of a family in a home and in the environment typical of the reservation. As stated before, twenty-three homes shelter unmarried mothers. Six of these lived in tar-paper shacks; fourteen in frame houses—two of the latter being classed as being very promiscuous—and three in rehabilitation houses. Twelve of the youth were addicted to intoxicating liquor. Four of them were young men, one living in a tar-paper shack, and three in frame houses. Of the eight young women so addicted, four lived in tar-paper shacks, two in frame houses, and two in reha-bilitation houses.

The third generation on the White Earth Reservation stands on the threshold of American civilization from which there is no escape, no turning back. Tribal life has all but lost its hold under economic pressure and the forces of a new social order. It is imperative that the Chippewa youth be given guidance and a secure footing in the best that the new social order has to offer.

SOURCES

1. Benj. G. Armstrong, *Early Life among the Indians* (Ashland: A. W. Bowron, 1892), p. 127.
2. Franz Pierz, *Die Indianer in Nord-Amerika, ihre Lebensweise, Sitten, Gebrauche, etc.* (St. Louis: Franz Saler & Co., 1855), p. 23, 27.
3. Frances Densmore, *Chippewa Customs* (U.S. Bureau of American Ethnology Bulletin 86 [1929]), p. 72.
4. N. H. Winchell, (ed.) *The Aborigines of Minnesota* (Minnesota Historical Society, 1911), p. 602.
5. Armstrong, *op. cit.*, p. 103–104.
6. *Op. cit.*, p. 24.
7. Joseph A. Gilfillan, *The Ojibways in Minnesota* (In Collections of the Minnesota Historical Society, IX [1901]), 84.
8. Pierz, *op. cit.*, p. 25.
9. *Op. cit.*, p. 73.
10. Densmore, *op. cit.*, p. 73; Gilfillan, *op. cit.*, p. 84.
    Frederick Webb Hodge, *Handbook of American Indians North of Mexico* (U.S. Bureau of American Ethnology Bulletin 30, Part 1, [1907]), p. 279.
11. Densmore, *op. cit.*, p. 73.
12. Gilfillan, *op. cit.*, p. 85.
    William Warren, *History of the Ojibways* (In Collections of the Minnesota Historical Society, V [1885]), p. 253–254.
13. George Copway, *The Traditional History and Characteristic Sketches of the Ojibway Nation* (Boston: Benj. B. Mussey, 1851), p. 98.
14. *Op. cit.*, p. 100.
15. W. J. Hoffman, *The Midē wiwin or "Grand Medicine Society" of the Ojibwa* (In Seventh Annual Report of the U.S. Bureau of American Ethnology, 1885–1886 [1891]), *passim.*
16. Copway, *op. cit.*, p. 137; Densmore, *op. cit.*, p. 151; Gilfillan, *op. cit.*, p. 75; Warren, *op.cit.*, p. 135.
    Sister M. Inez Hilger, "In the Early Days of Wisconsin, An Amalgamation of Chippewa and European Cultures," *Wisconsin Archeologist*, 16:41, June, 1936.

17. *U.S. House Executive Documents,* No. 247, 51st Congress, 1st Session,
    p. 13–34.
    Copway, *op. cit.,* p. 138; Pierz, *op. cit.,* p. 50.
18. Hilger, *op. cit.,* p. 43.
19. *U.S. House Doc.,* No. 247, p. 26.
20. Armstrong, *op. cit.,* p. 127.
21. *U.S. Statutes at Large,* Vol. 43, Ch. 233.

CHAPTER V

Living Conditions
of One Hundred Fifty
Chippewa Families

After having discussed the type of dwelling in which the one hundred fifty Chippewa families were living, and having studied the one hundred fifty families themselves, we wondered what the living conditions of the families were. Was there ample room in the homes for all? What household equipment was there? Was there any expression of personality in the homes? What were the economic resources? Was there any relationship between housing and living conditions of these families?

LIVING CONDITIONS IN GENERAL*

In discussing living conditions of the Chippewa, one needs to recall that four generations ago their ancestors lived in wigwams, in primitive ways if measured by the American standard of today. All lived in one-room dwellings, often in crowded conditions with little more household equipment than was absolutely necessary. Everyone in the community was tolerant of such conditions; in fact, few, if any, knew or appreciated a standard of living other than their own.

If the one hundred fifty families of this study are a fair sample, many of the families of the White Earth Reservation have never experienced any other standard than one which was not entirely unlike that of their parents, grandparents or great-grandparents. Most of the one hundred fifty homes were greatly overcrowded, many families living in one- or two-room hovels with consequent lack of privacy for parents and children.

Little opportunity, too, was being afforded them to learn by observation or experience the manner in which their own standard of living could be raised. If they had had the opportunity, they might have learnt

*For complete tabulations of findings discussed in Chapter V, see Appendix E.

a better standard by social contact with whites. But there was little social intermingling between the whites of a better standard on the White Earth Reservation and the Indians.

Schools, too, might have assisted in raising it. But the day schools, being largely rural schools, were not equipped to give instructions in better standards by demonstration and pupil participation. The boarding schools, on the other hand, by their very nature provided an artificial standard, being highly institutionalized. Some of them, too, were not adequately equipped, and others not socially minded enough, to do effective work in raising standards of living. In any event, there appears to be but a small carry-over from school into home.

The homes of the families were unattractive for the most part. They were crowded, were equipped with a minimum of household necessities, and offered little opportunity for spiritual expression. Some of them showed a fine sense of cleanliness and orderliness; others were repulsive in their filthiness being littered with dirty bits of both raw and cooked foods, sputum, and in some cases with excreta of children and animals. In a number of them one had difficulty wading through piles of bedding, clothing, boxes, refuse, dogs, and cats. In fifteen of the seventy-one tar-paper shacks one would willingly have shared a meal with the family; with twenty-five of them, not unless one were on the point of starvation. On the other hand, one would willingly have shared a meal with thirty of the frame-house dwellers; but with eight, only if one faced starvation. In five of the rehabilitation houses conditions were attractive; none of them were so filthy as to be repulsive. With the remaining one hundred fifty families, one would have been willing to eat a meal only if very hungry.

SIZE AND USE OF ROOMS

CUBIC AIR SPACE

The National Association of Housing Officials makes the following statement in its report entitled *A Housing Program for the United States:* "Health and reasonable comfort seem to require about 500 cubic feet in room space for each adult, and for this purpose two children are usually counted as one adult."[1] The Committee on the Hygiene of Housing of the American Public Health Association in its preliminary report entitled, "Basic principles of healthful housing," enumerates a set of principles, one of which reads: "Provision of an atmosphere of reasonable chemical purity." In the discussion of this principle, the committee says: "The important atmospheric impurities present in the home under ordinary conditions are those contributed by cooking, by various heat sources, and those derived from the human body. . . ." And then states that the cubic space per occupant in any occupied room should be four hundred cubic feet, but that where "the same room is used for both living and sleeping, the value should be increased to 500 cubic feet to allow for necessary furniture."[2] In its Introductory Statement, the same committee notes that the principles and specific requirements as formulated by them "are believed to be fundamental minima required for the promotion of physical, mental and social health, essential in low cost as well as in high cost housing, on the farm as well as in the city tenement."[3]

The homes of the one hundred fifty families fell far below the standards set by both of the above associations. The mean cubic feet of air space per person per room for the seventy-one families living in tar-paper shacks was 7.08; for the seventy-one in frame houses, 4.17; and for the eight in rehabilitation houses, 35.12. In fact, the mean number of cubic feet per person per *total* air space per dwelling for families living in tar-paper shacks was not very much in excess of the standard of five hundred cubic feet per person per room, being 880.9.

The mean for dwellers in frame houses was 1053.7 cubic feet per person per total air space per house; for rehabilitation homes, 842.6.

USE OF ROOMS

According to the American standards of living, a dwelling should have a minimum of six rooms. There should be a living-room for social intercourse of the family, a dining-room in which meals are served and a kitchen in which they are prepared, and at least three bedrooms for sleeping, one for the parents, one for the boys, and one for the girls. When these minimum requirements are not met, it is ordinarily assumed that they affect the environmental training of the children and the attitudes and morale of the family. Few of the Chippewa families met these standards. As noted in Chapter III, of the entire one hundred fifty homes only nine–all of them frame houses–had six or more rooms. In only three of them did a single family have six or more rooms, for six of the nine houses having six or more rooms were occupied by two families.

Moreover, it was found that of the seventy-one tar-paper shacks, fifty per cent consisted of one room only. Consequently in fifty per cent of them, one room served as living-room, dining-room, bedroom, and kitchen. Furthermore, a living-room, which is so essential to American living, did not exist in 89.4 per cent of the homes. The 10.6 per cent having one were all frame homes.

The Committee on the Hygiene of Housing considered opportunities for normal family life a fundamental psychological need. To quote: "Privacy is one element in normal family life; but sociability is another, which is psychologically and socially quite as important. Opportunity for adolescent youth to meet persons of the opposite sex under wholesome conditions should be provided. To meet these needs a common living-room which can be occupied by all members of the family, plus reasonable space elsewhere for withdrawal during periods of entertainment, would seem essential."[4] The above, then is a standard for the American people; but 89.4 per cent of the one hundred fifty families were without a living-room.

SLEEPING ARRANGEMENTS

Again, to quote from *A Housing Program for the United States*:

> There is much to be said for encouraging the provision of three bedrooms rather than one or two, even if the extra room must be small. Apart from the obvious need at times even in small families to divide the sexes, there arise in family life frequent occasions of sickness, births and deaths, and the need to accommodate a visitor, when the absence of any spare bedroom is a serious inconvenience. Moreover, with one living-room only, the opportunities for quiet reading or study on the part of the younger members of the family may depend on a small additional bedroom being available.[5]

In discussing adequate privacy for the individuals, under "Fundamental psychological needs," the Committee on the Hygiene of Housing states that a room shared with one person is an essential minimum, and continues, "Such a room should be occupied only by persons of the same sex except for married couples and young children. The age at which separation of sexes should occur is fixed by law in England at ten years, but some American authorities would place the figure at two years lower. Sleeping-rooms of children above the age of two years, according to psychiatric opinion, should be separate from those of parents."[6]

In discussing the provision of sufficient space in sleeping-rooms to minimize the danger of contact infections, the same committee advises at least a three-foot space between the beds, this distance preventing the spread of communicable diseases by means of mouth spray from an infected person.[7]

The above-named committees formulated the above-quoted standards as minima for the American people. The Chippewa Indians of the one hundred fifty families of this study met practically none of them.

They had little privacy, if any, and their sleeping conditions were exceedingly crowded. In only thirty-six of the one hundred fifty families did parents sleep without having one, two, or three children crowded into bed with them. Children often slept four, five, or six in a bed, in many instances resting crosswise on the bed or more often in two rows, one row with heads toward the upper and the other with heads toward the lower end of the bed. Pre-adolescent boys and girls often slept in the same bed; great care seemed to have been taken, however, not to allow adolescent boys and girls to do so.

CONCLUSIONS

In forty per cent of the homes (twenty-four per cent of the tar-paper shacks and sixteen per cent of the frame houses) parents had no privacy. Eighty-nine per cent of all rooms were being used for sleeping purposes, and as noted before, only three of all the families met the standard of a minimum of three bedrooms per family.

HOUSEHOLD EQUIPMENT

BEDS AND BEDDING

The beds of the early Chippewa were made on the ground of the wigwam or, during warm weather, often on the ground under the open sky. In the summer, beds consisted of cedar boughs covered with bulrush or cedar-bark mats. In the winter months, however, hides filled with feathers or deer hair were often placed on the mats. Coverings usually consisted of bear or deer hides, tanned with hair on them. The general practice, however, was not for bed mates to share coverings but for each member of the family to roll himself up in a separate fur hide.

A member of the family, adult as well as child, wishing to retire, removed his moccasins, retaining the rest of his day clothes, rolled himself up in his fur robe of deer or bear hide and lay on his mat with feet toward fire, covering his head and face completely and tightly with anything at hand. Each person, therefore, slept alone, rolled up in his fur robe, except husband and wife who shared theirs. When all were thus snug in their robes, much of the floor of the wigwam was occupied.

Although cedar boughs and rush mats had been replaced by bedsteads and springs in most of the one hundred fifty homes, fur robes had been merely replaced by blankets, each member of the family claiming his own. Day clothes, except shoes, were usually not removed and heads and faces were covered.

A whining child who was troublesome during an interview was told by the mother, "Go get your blanket and roll up and get to sleep!" A sick man was seen in his bed, rolled in a covering made of patched pieces of discarded clothing, with head and face completely covered by means of a turkish towel while his bare feet projected beyond the covering. A surprise visit in the morning found children rising from an old mattress on the floor, each child disentangling itself from its own blanket and needing only to slip on its shoes to be dressed for the day. A six-year-old girl at the Mission School related that she, her three sisters, and two brothers all slept in the same bed. "We girls each have our own blanket, but mama hasn't enough for all of us, so the boys have to roll up in one together." A mother in one of the families had gotten to dislike her husband because of the drinking he was doing and would, therefore, no longer share the blanket with him. "I roll up in my own blanket and he can roll up in his."

The old people insist that in the early days everybody was warm, and that it was an easy matter to supply the family with bedding. In many of the Chippewa homes of this study the supply of bedding was decidedly inadequate. Bedsteads were wanting in twenty-three of the families, for, in nine frame homes and fourteen tar-paper shacks, persons were sleeping on the floor. Although beds were usually of metal, twenty-five of them (five in frame houses, eighteen in tar-paper shacks and two in rehabilitation homes) were of wood and homemade. This was significant since many families had difficulty in combating bedbugs. Beds ranged from double beds in good condition to adjustable cots of little value. Almost without exception beds needed to be painted.

Most mattresses were of the regular commercial type and some were homemade consisting of cloth containers filled with feathers, deer hair, or straw. All persons in the one hundred fifty families, except several in four tar-paper shacks, slept on mattresses. Quilts and old coats were substitutes for mattresses for those who slept on the floor. All but five of the pillows owned by the families were filled with feathers, usually with feathers of wild fowl.

Comforters and blankets were greatly needed in all the homes. The temperature in the White Earth Reservation area, as may be recalled, is sub-zero from four to five months of the year, dropping as low as -50° at times. On an average there were fewer than two woolen coverings and blankets per family. Woolen coverings in most cases were made by stitching together pieces cut from discarded men's trousers and men's and women's coats. On cold nights, all heavy clothing owned by the family was used as coverings. Table XVI gives the mean for beds and bedding.

TABLE XVI

Mean for Beds and Bedding for One Hundred Fifty
Chippewa Indian Families on the White Earth Reservation in 1938

BEDS AND BEDDING	TAR-PAPER SHACK FAMILIES	FRAME-HOUSE FAMILIES	U.S. REHABILITATION-HOUSE FAMILIES
Beds	2.6	2.9	2.4
Mattresses	2.9	2.8	2.8
Pillows	3.3	3.4	5.5
Woolen coverings	.5	1.8	.7
Cotton coverings	3.8	5.6	6.1

CONCLUSIONS

The number of beds, mattresses, and pillows found in the families was
not related to housing; but the number of families, some of whose members were sleeping on the floor, was definitely related to tar-paper
shacks. Frame-house dwellers were better supplied in both woolen and
cotton comforters and blankets than were tar-paper shacks.

BED LINENS, TOWELS, AND TABLECLOTHS

Bed linens, towels, and tablecloths were unknown to the traditional
Chippewa housekeeper, for cloth was not known to them. Furs served
as bedding. Towels were hardly needed, for washing consisted of bathing
in rivers and lakes, and drying oneself in wind and sun. The wooden and
birch-bark dishes were never washed. Tablecloths were not needed, for
meals were eaten off bulrush mats spread on the floor.

Although bed linens, towels, and tablecloths were found in some of
the one hundred fifty homes, in most of them there was a dearth of
household linens. The following table shows the findings regarding bed
linens, towels, and tablecloths.

TABLE XVII

Bed Linens, Face Towels, and Tablecloths in the Homes of One Hundred Fifty
Chippewa Indian Families on the White Earth Reservation in 1938

ITEMS	TAR-PAPER SHACK FAMILIES	FRAME-HOUSE FAMILIES	U.S. REHABILITATION - HOUSE FAMILIES	ALL ITEMS
Bed linens				
No sheets	15	2	1	18
Fewer than six sheets	54	60	4	118
No pillow slips	5	2	1	8
Fewer than six pillow slips	47	34	2	83
Face towels				
None	1	–	–	1
Fewer than six	57	26	3	86
Tablecloths				
None	11	7	1	19
Oilcloth	59	61	4	124
Cloth cover	2	6	3	11
Linoleum	2	–	–	2

It was thought that six sheets should be the minimum for each household, since most families required at least three beds, one for parents, and one each for girls and boys. (It was taken for granted that sheets and slips be washed and replaced on the beds in a day.) If worn-out cotton blankets, sheets made of flour sacks, bedspreads, and calico cloth intended for quilt coverings were not counted as sheets, the number of families not having any would be greatly increased.

Eighty-six of the families had fewer than six towels, one in a tar-paper shack not having any. In some cases towels had been brought home from boarding school, the printed name of the child still being visible on the towel.

CONCLUSIONS

The possession of household linens was definitely associated with houses. Dwellers in frame houses exceeded tar-paper shack people in all counts except in the number of families who had fewer than six sheets and who had oilcloth table coverings, and in them the differences were small.

KITCHEN UTENSILS, TABLE SERVICE, STORAGE PLACE FOR BOTH

Kitchen utensils in the early day consisted of kettles, wooden spoons, and bone knives. None of the informants recalled hearing what utensil was used in place of iron kettles in the early day. Kettles were suspended from tripods, or from a pole that rested in the crotches of two saplings thrust into the ground, in upright position, several feet apart. Large wooden spoons were made by scraping and burning the knot of a soft-wood tree. Knives were made from the flat rib bones of the moose, deer, and buffalo.

Table service consisted of non-leakable cups made of folded birch bark; of shallow birch-bark trays, usually leakable because of holes made in stitching them;[8] of wooden bowls made from knots of hardwood trees; and of small wooden spoons.

Cooking utensils and table service were usually stored by being piled into each other, or upon each other, in a place to the right of the entrance of the wigwam.

American housewives today consider certain kitchen utensils and table service indispensable. Among the indispensable kitchen utensils are frying pans, roasters, kettles and pans for boiling or stewing foods, bread mixing pans, bread tins, pie tins, a coffee pot, a tea pot, a butcher knife and a paring knife. Among the table service are a plate, cup, saucer, dessert dish, and drinking glass for each member of the family, as well as salt and pepper shakers, vegetable dishes and platters for serving food. Table XVIII lists the number of families who were without these articles.

TABLE XVIII

Kitchen Utensils and Table Service in the Homes of One Hundred Fifty
Chippewa Indian Families on the White Earth Reservation in 1938

ITEMS	TAR-PAPER SHACK FAMILIES	FRAME-HOUSE FAMILIES	U.S. REHABILITATION-HOUSE FAMILIES	ALL ITEMS
Kitchen utensils (families not having any)				
Frying pans	10	19	2	31
Roasters	53	37	4	94
Kettles and cooking pans	2	–	–	2
Coffee pots	5	2	–	7
Tea pots	25	36	1	62
Tea kettles	26	13	2	41
Bread-mixing pan or dish pan	26	17	3	46
Bread tins	12	7	1	20

TABLE XVIII *(continued)*

ITEMS	TAR-PAPER SHACK FAMILIES	FRAME-HOUSE FAMILIES	U.S. REHABILITATION - HOUSE FAMILIES	ALL ITEMS
Pie tins	18	7	–	25
Butcher knives	1	1	–	2
Paring knives	31	27	3	61
Water pails	2	–	–	2
Table service (families not having any)				
Saucers	25	9	1	35
Dessert dishes	44	26	2	72
Vegetable dishes	25	16	2	43
Platters	28	14	1	43
Salt and pepper shakers	5	3	2	10
Water glasses	15	12	–	27

Cooking kettles, coffee pots, or tea pots were often replaced by quart or gallon syrup pails, by gallon or smaller cans emptied of their canned products, by marshmallow or National Biscuit Company cans. Dish pans were used by most of the families for mixing bread; bread was often baked in frying pans, cooking pans, or any pan or low metal dish.

Nearly each member of the one hundred fifty families was supplied with a plate and cup, or some substitute for them. Substitutes for plates were usually pie tins, while those for cups were mayonnaise dressing jars or tin cans of pint size. Many homes had enamelled dishes.

Cooking utensils were usually hung on pegs near the stove, or were left standing on the stove. If the home was provided with a pantry, however, both cooking and table service were stored in it. All rehabilitation houses but only two frame houses and one tar-paper shack had pantries. All families but six (three in frame houses and three in tar-paper shacks) had kitchen cabinets or cupboards in which to store dishes and supplies; six merely stored them on an extra table found in the kitchen. The cabinet and cupboards ranged from homemade, open shelves to some of the best that Montgomery Ward sold.

CONCLUSIONS

The seventy-one tar-paper shack families had fewer, than did frame-house people, of all kitchen utensils and table service considered essential by American families. There was little relationship between housing and facilities for storing utensils, dishes, and food, for only two of the frame-house families and one of the tar-paper shacks had pantries; an equal number in each group had cabinets or cupboards.

HEATING AND COOKING APPARATUS: HEATERS, STOVES, FUEL, OUTDOOR FIRES

Wigwams in the early day were heated by open fires located in a shallow pit in the center of the wigwam. If the wigwam was large and two families occupied it, there might have been two fireplaces on the center line, one in each half of the wigwam. Smoke was emitted through the roof, directly over the fireplace, by means of a draft created by the manner in which the rush mats, which were used to prevent the cold from blowing in on people, were placed against the wall of the interior.[9] The fireplace served also for cooking purposes. A tripod of green saplings was placed over it, and from the junction of these, crotched twigs with hooks were hung for holding cooking utensils. Firewood which produced most heat and least smoke—alder wood being best—was collected by the women each day, a supply of wood seldom being at hand.

Sixty-three of the one hundred fifty families (twenty-two in frame houses, forty in tar-paper shacks, and one in a rehabilitation house) built outdoor fires. Fourteen used tripods like the ones used indoors in the early day, five of the families so doing lived in frame houses and nine in tar-paper shacks. Eighteen used another traditional outdoor type. It was made by resting a pole in the crotches of two saplings which had been stoutly fastened into the ground in an upright position, the distance between these saplings being five to eight feet. One woman adhered to the method used in the earlier day when en route. It consisted of a green sapling securely wedged into the ground with one end while the other leaned over the fire. Thirty-one of the families (ten in frame houses, twenty in tar-paper shacks, and one in a rehabilitation house) built outside fires under grates or in discarded stoves.

All but one of the families had kitchen stoves, one family having recently lost its because of neglect in meeting payments. The stoves ranked from the very best made—seventeen of which were still being paid for (twelve in frame houses, three in tar-paper shacks and two in rehabilitation houses)—to those that were so broken that eight (two in frame houses and six in tar-paper shacks) could not be used for baking. One family used a heater for cooking.

In fifty-eight homes (nineteen frame houses, thirty-eight tar-paper shacks, and one rehabilitation house) kitchen stoves were the only heaters for the home. Two families in frame houses had furnaces. The remaining homes had heaters of various types and sizes. In seven of the tar-paper shacks, fifty-gallon oil cans had been ingeniously designed by the owners to serve as the "best heaters we ever had." A hole was cut in one end of the barrel and a door of a discarded stove was attached so as to close the opening at that end. Four metal legs of discarded stoves or several bricks piled upon each other served as braces. Smoke was emitted by means of stove pipes neatly tacked on the upper section of the can at the end opposite the door.

One hundred six of the families (forty-six in frame houses, fifty-four in tar-paper shacks, and six in rehabilitation houses) gathered their own wood at not any, or only a small, cost. Forty-four (twenty-five in frame houses, seventeen in tar-paper shacks, and two in rehabilitation houses) bought their wood. The remaining families bought some and gathered some.

Ten of the families (nine in frame houses and one in a tar-paper shack) used kerosene stoves when the supply of firewood gave out or during the hot days of summer. Two of the families in Waubun burned coal.

CONCLUSIONS

A relationship existed between housing and methods and manner of cooking and heating. Frame houses led by nine in the number who had bought new stoves and were still paying for them; in furnaces, for the only two homes having them were frame houses; by eight for families buying all their fuel; by eight in the possession of kerosene stoves. Tar-paper shacks led by six in the stoves that could not be used for baking; by nineteen in the homes whose stoves were the only heaters; in oil-drum heaters, being the only ones using them; by eight in the gathering of all fuel used by them; by eighteen in the traditional use of outdoor fires; by twenty in the use of grates for outdoor cooking.

TABLES AND WRITING DESKS

Tables of wood were unknown to the old Chippewa. Bulrush mats spread on the ground served as their dining-room tables; tanned buckskin spread on the ground as kitchen tables; and they had need of none other.

One first-generation couple still ate its meals off bulrush mats although it owned a table. "My old woman and I like our food best when we can eat it the old Indian way." The remaining families, however, used tables. Tables were either homemade or factory-made. The homemade ones, built of rough lumber, were made by the men as a rule, although in several instances the women remarked that they had made them. Seventy-one of the families (twenty-eight in frame houses, forty-two in tar-paper shacks, and one in a rehabilitation house) had homemade tables, while seventy-nine (forty-three in frame houses, twenty-nine in tar-paper shacks and seven in rehabilitation houses) had factory-made ones. Fifteen of the families owned writing tables of some sort, twelve of these lived in frame houses and three in tar-paper shacks.

Tables were not always large enough to accommodate the entire family at meal time, nor were there chairs or substitutes for chairs for each member. Lacking table space and chairs, as well as dishes, some families simply set all food on the table, and members who happened to be at hand seated themselves and left as finished, others merely taking their places and using their unwashed dishes. In other families, where table space, dishes, or chairs were insufficient, members carried their food in whatever dish was available and ate it sitting on the floor, resting backs against walls. A number were seen eating their food outdoors while lounging in the shade of a tree. If one had not been aware of the fact that this was an everyday occurrence, one would have thought these families were enjoying a picnic!

CONCLUSIONS

The possession of tables was not related to housing, but the type of table was. Frame houses exceeded tar-paper shacks by fifteen in factory-made tables and by nine in writing desks, while tar-paper shacks exceeded frame houses by fourteen in homemade tables.

CHAIRS

In their primitive culture, the Chippewa had no chairs nor an elevated object of any kind used for sitting. They squatted on rush mats, or furs, or on the bare ground when at work or when eating, and lounged on them while at leisure.

Although there was still much squatting by the first and second generation when at work, and much lounging by all when not at work, nearly all homes had chairs or substitutes for them. All but twenty-four of the families had chairs, eight of these twenty-four lived in frame houses, while sixteen lived in tar-paper shacks. Frame-house dwellers, too, had a larger number of rockers or armchairs. Of the eighty-one families having them, forty-nine lived in frame houses, twenty-seven in tar-paper shacks, and five in rehabilitation houses. Although some rockers were in good condition, most of them were lacking some part. A few homes had upholstered armchairs, remnants of the boom days of allotment or timber sales. Backless chairs were found in forty-nine of the homes (twenty-one frame houses and twenty-eight tar-paper shacks).

Substitutes for chairs were benches, wooden grocery-boxes, metal lard cans, nail kegs, trunks, and edges of beds. All benches were home-made of unfinished lumber gotten at nearby mills and showed unskilled workmanship. Some were one-seated; others seated three or four adults. Eighty-four of the homes (thirty-eight frame houses, forty-five tar-paper shacks, and one a rehabilitation house) owned benches. Thirty-four of the families (twelve in frame houses, twenty-one in tar-paper shacks, and one in a rehabilitation house) used substitutes for chairs.

In one home, two benches were improvised at mealtime by placing planks across milk cans. Wooden boxes, such as groceries are shipped in, were used by some of the families. Three families at Mahnomen considered themselves fortunate in having gotten fifty-pound metal lard cans from one of the butcher shops. "We have our bids in for more," said one mother. "They make fine chairs and wash boilers. My mother in Beaulieu wants one to use as a boiler." One family in a rehabilitation house had nailed boards over two neatly painted nail kegs, thus forming a bench.

CONCLUSIONS

The possession of chairs and the type of chairs were related to housing, for frame-house dwellers exceeded tar-paper shacks in possession of rockers and chairs. Tar-paper shacks exceeded frame houses in backless chairs and in substitutes for chairs.

LAUNDRY APPARATUS

In the early days, the Chippewa women did their washing by rubbing it with both hands on the shores of rivers or lakes, and drying it on tall grass or underbrush.

Very few of the one hundred fifty families washed by hand, and washing in rivers or lakes was not done except when in the rice fields, when berry-picking, or when in sugar bushes away from home. Most families had wash tubs and wash boards; some had boilers and some had washing machines; most of them had permanent wash lines. Only forty-four of the families owned washing machines (twenty-four in frame houses, seventeen in tar-paper shacks and three in rehabilitation houses). Four of the machines were worked by hand power and thirty-five of them were operated by gasoline engines.

Sixteen of the washing machines were still being paid for (eight by frame-house dwellers, six by tar-paper shack people and two by rehabilitation house occupants). Twenty-eight of the owners of the machines lived in the villages of White Earth, Naytahwaush, Beaulieu, and in the town of Mahnomen. One was led to infer that some high-powered salesman had been through the community, when one found several expensive machines, ranging in price from $75.00 to $150.00, in homes poorly equipped in even the essentials of good housekeeping. In two of the families there were six and seven members each with no income except the father's W.P.A. bi-weekly check of $22.00. The collector appeared promptly on the day installment payments were due. "I always have the money for him too; I won't slip up on that, for I don't want to lose the washmachine," said one woman. Another had not reckoned on the cost of gasoline when she purchased hers. "But I drain my old man's car if he doesn't buy me the gasoline. It's just as good running my washmachine as it is taking him to the beer joints," she noted. Another would not part with hers, although she did not have sufficient cooking utensils, bed linens, and comforters. The interior of her house, too, needed repair badly. "But," she remarked, "I'll pay for the machine first and then we'll have these holes in the floor boarded over. Probably we can get that done next year. We were pestered plenty by rats last winter but we'll have to put up with them again this winter."

Five of the families living in towns where electricity is available (four in frame houses and one in a tar-paper shack) had washing machines run by electricity. Very few of the families had a wash boiler. Families having washing machines noted that they needed no boiler while others used fifty-pound lard cans, dish pans or pails, or in the summer large black kettles over an outdoor fire, in which to boil wash. Many did not boil their wash.

Three of the families in frame houses had cisterns, while two in tar-paper shacks used lake water for washing. The remaining families caught rain water by means of boards or troughs, having one end of these attached to a corner of the eaves while the other rested in a barrel or wash tub or some container. When rain water gave out, hard water was used. In the winter months snow was usually melted.

With the above equipment, it was difficult for the families to keep clean, and yet some did so unusually well. One mother remarked, "Yes, my children and my house are clean, but I'm worn out trying to keep them so. We haven't much money to spend on soap, and then, too, it's quite a ways to haul the water up here from the lake; our well water is too hard to be used for washing. There was a fellow here trying to sell me one of those gasoline washmachines, but I told him I couldn't even afford to get a wringer!" Only two of the families had wringers, not including those who had them attached to washing machines.

CONCLUSIONS

There was only a slight relationship between ownership of accessories for washing clothes and housing. Families living in frame houses exceeded tar-paper shack dwellers by seven in ownership of washing machines; but sixty per cent of all families were without them.

SEWING MACHINES

Implements used for sewing, in traditional days, were the bone awl or the thorns of the thorn-apple tree and thread of sinew or vegetable fiber. The bone awl or thorns were used in piercing leather; sinew of the deer, elk, and moose, or the fibers of the basswood tree or nettle stalk, were used as thread. The sinew, especially that of the elk and deer, could be split into exceedingly fine strands. Beadworkers in the one hundred fifty families in making buckskin clothes, gloves, or moccasins still used sinew, but bone awls had been replaced by metal ones.

In doing the family sewing, women used steel needles, cotton or silk thread, and sewing machines. Eighty of the families (forty-two in frame houses, thirty-five in tar-paper shacks, and three in rehabilitation houses) owned a sewing machine, two of the women in tar-paper shacks having borrowed their mothers' to do the children's sewing. "I go down to mother's to use her machine and she and I do my kids' sewing together." "I can stitch fine but can't cut," said one young mother. Homemakers' clubs and women's W.P.A. projects had taught some of the women to sew new clothes and to remodel old ones. Three of the mothers (two in tar-paper shacks and one in a frame house) were still paying on recently purchased machines, the machines being new ones.

CONCLUSIONS

Frame-house dwellers exceeded those of tar-paper shacks by seven in the ownership of sewing machines.

ARTIFICIAL LIGHT

The fireplace in the wigwam gave sufficient light for ordinary work to the Chippewa family of the early day. In the summer months, no light was needed, ordinarily, for the end of dusk was bedtime; during the winter months, however, the evenings were spent in visiting and in story telling for both entertainment and instruction. Old men or women, often on invitation, told the traditional stories and the historic events of the tribe to those who lounged around in the wigwam on rush mats or on their beds of fur. Stories which contained lessons for children and youth were part of the evening program from the first snowfall in winter to the first thunderclap in the spring.

If a woman's work required a light, she twisted a piece of birch bark tightly, stuck it into a piece of wood and set all upright into the ground. In the event that light was needed outside the wigwam, a lighted piece of birch bark served as a torch of short duration, while a cornucopia of bark filled with resin and bits of birch bark served for longer periods, such as the time needed for the fetching of one skilled in herbs to the bedside of a sick member of the family.

Today kerosene and gasoline lamps or electric lights are used by the Chippewa. Of the one hundred fifty families, nine frame-house dwellers who lived in towns where electricity was available were using electric lights; one was using gasoline. All others used kerosene lamps. Gas lamps are dangerous and require knowledge as to lighting and for these reasons were not favored by the Indians.

CONCLUSIONS

No relationship existed between housing and lighting of homes. This was largely due to force of circumstances, electricity not being available to the larger number of families.

TELLING TIME

The Chippewa in their old culture had little need of knowing the exact time of the day. Sunrise was the signal to be up; or possibly dawn, in the event that journeys had to be made. Meals were served whenever the family was hungry or whenever the supply of fresh meat or fish was brought in. No one needed to be at work or meet an appointment at a very exact time; patient waiting is one of the virtues of the Indian. Those who did feel the need of knowing the time of day rather accurately laid out a sundial anywhere on bare ground in an open space. Sundials, such as were used in the early day, are occasionally used today.

Sundials, to-day, are used primarily when camping away from home and are still made in the same manner as in early days. On a clear night a man will stake a stick, about a yard high, and lying flat on the ground move about until the stick and the north star are in line. A second stick of about the same length will then be laid to the south of the first stick and in line with it and the north star, and be staked about a yard from the first. (An informant on the Lac Courte Orielle Reservation did not stake a second stick but simply drew a straight line north and south through the first stick.) In the morning a line is drawn through the base of the south stick at right angles to the line of the two sticks. When the shadow of the south stick falls on the westerly line it is about six o'clock in the morning; when it falls in line with the north stick, it is noonday; when on the easterly line it is nearly six o'clock in the evening. The remaining hours of the day are only approximately read.

The method used by an old Indian at Red Lake varies somewhat from the above. Two sticks are staked as described above. In the morning, a third one is staked to the south and in line with the first two. A semi-circle is then drawn through the third stick, convex to the southward. When the shadow of the third stick falls west and tangent to the circle, it is approximately six in the morning; when it falls in line with the two sticks to the north, it is noonday; when, to the east and tangent to the circle, it is approximately six in the evening.[10]

Today the Chippewa tell time in the modern way. All but four of the one hundred fifty families had modern ways of telling time; the four, all living in tar-paper shacks, relied on neighbors' clocks, in case the need for knowing time arose. One hundred twenty-eight of the families (sixty-one in frame houses, sixty in tar-paper shacks, and seven in rehabilitation houses) used alarm clocks. Alarm clocks were favored because they were both cheap and could be used to announce the hour for rising. The Chippewa of today must be at work on scheduled time. Five in each group had mantel clocks; three of the frame-house dwellers had wall clocks. Five of the families (four in frame houses and one in a tar-paper shack) had to rely on a watch of some member of the family.

CONCLUSIONS

The possession of a time piece was only slightly related to housing. Of the tar-paper shack dwellers, four owned no time piece while four others had to rely on someone's watch. All wall clocks were owned by frame-house people. There was no significant difference between the groups in ownership of alarm clocks, and none in the ownership of mantel clocks.

STORAGE FACILITIES

STORAGE OF FOODS

In traditional days dried berries and fresh and dried vegetables were stored in caches. Although no caches were found among the families of this study, some were found on other Chippewa reservations in the summers of ethnological study. The writer witnessed the opening of one such cache on the Red Lake Reservation by Old Lady Badboy, eighty-two years of age, on August 1, 1933. An Indian offered her $1.00 for a bushel of potatoes from her garden, to which she rejoined that they were not full-grown; but that she would be willing, at that price, to sell some of last year's. She proceeded to a grove of maple trees near her one-room house and from a place in it began to remove some saplings she had felled and placed there the previous fall. She next lifted off several armfuls of cornstocks, and then some dead leaves. All of this, she noted, was needed to "fool" the deer. "Deer won't walk on dead trees for their feet catch in them. Without these trees, they can find the cache by the feel of their feet. Any soft spot raises their suspicions," she remarked. She next removed hay to about the depth of one foot and then lifted out several rutabagas and finally a bushel of good-sized, fine, healthy looking potatoes. The cache was six feet deep and about three feet square. The outer walls were lined with hay to about the depth of eight inches. "I had three of these filled with vegetables from my gardens last fall," she said with legitimate pride. She then took us to see the cache in which she was storing blueberries and gooseberries of the summer's canning. The Mason fruit jars containing them were so placed that each jar could be surrounded with hay. "I have stored my canned things that way ever since we learnt to put up things in glass jars and I have never had any of them freeze. The food I need for winter I keep in my house; whatever I put in the caches stays there until the snow melts. That's the hardest time of all the year. Indians that didn't provide for themselves in the fall often nearly starve in the late winter. I belong to the Pembina band, and it was seldom heard, when we still lived the Indian way, that any of us were starving."

As noted before, none of the families of our study made use of caches in the open, but one is inclined to think of their so-called cellars—which were mere dug-outs—as caches underneath their houses. Eighty of the one hundred fifty houses had a place under some part of the house to which the name cellar was given. In only four of them, however, were the walls supported by cement or lumber and were they deep enough that one could walk in them. The depth of sixty-three of the eighty cellars was five feet, while the floor space was three feet square; the remaining seventeen varied in all dimensions, none being higher than six feet and longer than seven. All of the rehabilitation houses and some of the frame houses and tar-paper shacks had steps leading into these cellars; others, one entered by dropping down a chair or, oftener still, by dropping oneself down. "As to the size of my cellar, it's not very big. You can lift that trapdoor and see for yourself. I myself can't get through the door, and if I could I'd fill up the whole cellar," said one woman. "Yes, you're right," added her husband, "that cellar is five by three by three! But that's the only kind of cellar anybody around here has. We store potatoes in ours." Several families kept canned food in theirs; most of them stored vegetables for winter use, especially potatoes.

There may have been several reasons for these small storage places. Most families lived on a subsistence standard the year around and seldom had surplus foods. Their garden produce, canned or raw, was the only commodity that needed to be stored and a comparatively small number raised enough for storage. Again, very few families were able to procure lumber or cement to build proper homes, much less to build cellars. A third reason probably lay in their traditions.

CONCLUSIONS

Of the eighty families using cellars, twenty-seven lived in tar-paper shacks, forty-five in frame houses, and eight in rehabilitation houses. Although the frame houses exceeded tar-paper shacks by eighteen in number having cellars, it was interesting to find tar-paper shacks having cellars at all, since none of them had either a stone or a cement foundation, and consequently the freezing of vegetables might readily be expected.

STORAGE OF CLOTHES AND OTHER EFFECTS

Tribal custom did not require more than one attire for each person. Men, women, and children, in traditional days, wore buckskin clothing made of finely tanned hides of deer, reindeer, moose, bear, and elk, and of delicately dressed skins of rabbit, beaver, weasel, and other small animals. The men's costume consisted of breechcloth, leggings, moccasins, and a blanket; that of the women, of a single garment made of two deerskins—one forming the front, the other the back—and of leggings and moccasins. No storage space was needed for clothing for one costume was worn on all occasions, it being replaced only when worn-out. Several pairs of moccasins, however, were always on hand, and so were tanned skins. These and any personal belongings, such as bows and arrows, sewing material, etc., were stored in rolls of birch bark or in woven bags of cedar bark, and were placed along the walls of the wigwam. Some families, also had bark lodges close to the home wigwam in which personal belongings and implements were stored. Several of these were seen on the Red Lake and Lac du Flambeau reservations.

In more recent times the Chippewa, as all other Americans, found that storage places for clothes were a necessity. In the one hundred fifty homes, clothes were hung on pegs or lines and stored in trunks, dresser drawers, drawer chests, or open shelves; in piles in corners of rooms; in garages or storage houses; and in boxes in corners or under beds. Some families took great care to store clothes away neatly and carefully. If no other facilities were available, lines were strung across corners, and dresses, coats, suits, etc., were neatly hung on them over hangers made from bent willow twigs, crooked nails serving as hooks. In many instances the line of clothes was covered with a piece of cloth to keep out dust. Table XIX lists the facilities for storage found in the homes.

TABLE XIX

Facilities for Storage of Clothes and Other Effects of One Hundred Fifty Chippewa Indian Families on the White Earth Reservation in 1938

STORAGE FACILITIES	TAR-PAPER SHACK FAMILIES	FRAME-HOUSE FAMILIES	U.S. REHABILITATION-HOUSE FAMILIES	ALL ITEMS
Lines strung across corners	39	29	1	69
Pegs driven into walls	51	53	1	105
Inbuilt clothes closets	8	15	8	31
Trunks	42	50	5	97
Dressers	30	52	5	87
Drawer chests	9	13	–	22
Open shelves	24	37	–	61
Storage houses	17	18	3	38
Attics	6	22	5	33

Most homes, not having ample storage place, looked disorderly. Many families had things piled up in corners and few were the homes in which clothing and other articles were not stored in boxes or travelling bags, boxes and bags invariably resting under beds. If the mother wanted the visitor to see a child's dress she had made at homemakers' club, or a crazy-patch quilt she was making, or possibly a bit of bead-work that had been made by her grandmother "before the whites ever came in here," or perhaps a snap shot of a little daughter that was in St. Paul with an aunt "who really adopted her but not by law," some child was sent crawling under the bed to pull out the proper box.

Trunks were favorite storage places. Open shelves in many instances were under the smoke exit of the chimney. The storage houses varied in sizes from small chicken coops to one-car garages.

CONCLUSIONS

Although nearly all homes needed more storage spaces, tar-paper shacks were in greater need of them than were frame houses. Frame houses exceeded tar-paper shacks in number of families having them by eight in trunks, twelve in dressers, four in drawer chests, thirteen in open shelves, one in storage houses, and sixteen in attics.

EXPRESSIONS OF PERSONALITY

INTERIOR DECORATION OF HOMES: ARTICLES OF CHIPPEWA CULTURE, FLOWERS, NEEDLECRAFT, BRAIDED RUGS, PHOTOGRAPHS, PRINTS, RELIGIOUS ARTICLES, ETC.

Traditionally the artistic temperament of the Chippewa found expression in beadwork, quill work, birch bark, and reeds. No pieces of art, however, were made merely to be used as wall decorations. All art was applied to useful articles, and these were seen about the wigwam.

Beadwork was applied to beautify tanned hides that were used as articles of clothing or on bags that were used for carrying or for storage purposes. The oldest patterns used in beadwork were those of geometric and angular designs. Such a design was made by folding and refolding a thin layer of birch bark and indenting it with the teeth in various ways; the unfolded bark in transparency showed a symmetrical design. Old women tell of the beautiful designs they used to make, "when I still had my teeth and when everybody was wearing beadwork." Today patterns are cut in a similar manner with scissors and folded paper, but are rarely used in beadwork. Several women, with a good deal of pride, showed comforters in which such designs had been worked out. Beadwork patterns today are largely conventional floral designs.

Birch-bark baskets or containers were often decorated with designs; thus a *makuk* (container for maple sugar) might have a fine spray of maple leaves designed on it. The design was drawn on the container after the latter had been soaked in water for a day or two, following which all the bark, excepting the design, was scraped off its top layer. When the bark was dry all but the design appeared in darker hue, thus giving the design some prominence. Four mothers and several children of the one hundred fifty families were making birch-bark bird houses and baskets for tourist trade in the summer of 1938. None were making any designs on them, however, "for tourists don't like to pay too much for them."

In the early days porcupine quills were dyed and used for decorative purposes on buckskin and birch bark. None of the White Earth Indians were doing quill work in the summer of 1938.

Occasionally one still sees rush mats such as were used in the early day either at mealtime or as beds. The colored pattern of diamonds made by using colored rushes is seldom seen, however. Generally no artistic design is used, borders of colored reeds making them attractive. Dyes for reeds were formerly made from vegetable matter, such as the bark and twigs of the alder, sumac, bloodroot, plum, oak or dogwood, and of mineral matter, such as is found in certain dry soils or at surface-flowing springs. Today, the lead of an indelible pencil is used.

Reed mats were not only being used in several of the homes included in this study but an old couple were pulling reeds to make mats. "We like to sit on mats in the summer," they said. Some women on the White Earth Reservation, too, were making sweet-grass baskets but without design or dye.

Traditional art, therefore, seemed almost completely gone from the White Earth Reservation and that brought by the white man was conspicuously absent in the homes. Although both tar-paper shacks and frame houses can be characterized as groups, one might step from a wigwam into some of the shacks and then into frame houses of unfinished interior, and hardly know that one had been in three types of houses, if one considered only the interior decoration of the houses. From the rafters, or at their junction with the wall, one might see hanging bunches of various sizes of medicinal herbs and roots, wrapping cord, bundles of basswood fiber, or perhaps strips of sinew, baby's shoes and stockings, a rosary or two, and some palm. Across one corner one might find a baby hammock of Chippewa type which was made by folding sides of a blanket over two ropes with the baby resting in the blanket between the ropes. On the walls, photographs of various sizes, colored prints of persons and nature, a calendar, a crucifix or some picture of Christ or the Saints might be seen; and on some dresser, drawer chest, sewing machine, or box, probably a statue of Christ or a Saint. Where walls met rafters a gun or two might be resting on long nails or pegs. Rarely would one see articles of traditional beadwork or birch bark or flowers either fresh, potted, or artificial. Needlework was a rarity. Kitchen utensils were seen hanging on pegs near the stove, while clothes were hanging on pegs on the wall or on lines stretched across corners.

Even when walls and ceilings were finished, the appearance of the homes differed little from the above except that nothing could be suspended from rafters and more was found hanging from walls. Rehabilitation houses, too, offered little variation.

The above description is typical of a Chippewa home and similar ones can be found in every community. However, many of the one hundred fifty homes deviated in one or several particulars, and certain particulars seemed to characterize the tar-paper shacks and the frame houses as groups.

Tar-paper shacks led in the retention of tribal characteristics, for dwellers in thirty-seven homes, or a few more than half, owned Chippewa articles, such as beadwork, moccasins, entire beaded buckskin suits, or Midē wiwin drums. Four of the families in tar-paper shacks, too, owned birch-bark articles such as baskets or trays, while none in the frame or rehabilitation houses did. Fourteen of the tar-paper shack dwellers had gathered medicinal herbs and roots; only two of the frame houses and none of the rehabilitation dwellers had. Twenty of the tar-paper shack dwellers had hides to tan, while only two of the frame-house dwellers did.

Although this survey was made during the season of wild flowers—and beautiful wild flowers of many varieties could easily have been had—none were found in any tar-paper shack nor rehabilitation house, and in only four frame houses. Fifteen of the frame houses, twelve of the tar-paper shacks, and two of the rehabilitation houses had bouquets of garden flowers. Twelve of the frame houses, one of the rehabilitation houses, and seven of the tar-paper shacks had potted flowers; while six of the frame houses and three of the tar-paper shacks had bouquets of artificial flowers.

The interior of the homes were drab, practically none of them being painted or wall-papered. Bouquets of flowers, therefore, would have added cheer to them. The old culture, said one old woman, did not permit the Chippewa to destroy anything of nature wantonly, and plucking wild flowers for no other use than that of keeping them in the house for a day or two savored of wanton destruction.

Although a fairly large percentage of the women had attended boarding schools—and in most boarding schools needlecraft was taught either as an art or as a leisure-time activity—only a few more than one-third (thirty-two of the frame-house, twenty-three of the tar-paper shack, and four of the rehabilitation-house dwellers) were using a piece of needlework for decorative purposes, while only about one-sixth (sixteen of the frame-houses, eight of the tar-paper shacks, and three of the rehabilitation-house dwellers) had a lounging pillow. While practically all of the women admitted that they had learnt needlecraft, only two of those who had been at boarding school had brought home with them a piece of work which they had made while at school. "Whatever we made stayed at the school," was a common answer. One wonders if it would not be well, in a new adaptation of the curriculum for Indian schools to Indian needs, to provide for the retention and for use in their own homes of at least some of the decorative needlework made by the girls. Or better still, might they not be encouraged to adapt their needlework and sewing to the needs of their homes?

Seventy-nine families, a few more than half (thirty-five in tar-paper shacks, thirty-eight in frame houses, and six in rehabilitation homes) had homemade, braided rag rugs, some of which showed fine color combinations. A few of the homes had drapes or curtains made of flour sacks or prints which added much to the attractiveness of the homes. In most homes, however, curtains and drapes were conspicuously absent.

On entering most homes, one noticed on the walls enlarged, often colored photographs in rather expensive frames. Any interest in them solicited a remark from parent or relative that these were pictures of deceased relatives or family members. Sixty-eight homes (thirty-eight frame houses, twenty-seven tar-paper shacks, and three rehabilitation houses) had such enlarged photographs. The memory of their dead is long and lovingly retained by the Chippewa. Those of the old culture never utter the given name of the dead but speak of them as "my deceased husband," "my dead child," etc. Formerly the mourners grieved over their loss for a year by dressing carelessly and loosening the hair so it fell over their shoulders. Then, as well as today, they placed food on their graves.

On the walls of twenty-nine of the frame houses, twenty-one of the tar-paper shacks, and three of the rehabilitation houses a number of snap shots of friends and of family members were crowded into frames, and stories told about the events of their taking. Nearly all homes had calendars. About two-thirds of the homes of each group had colored prints, such as are found on calendars, railroad advertisements, etc., tacked on walls. Sixty-six of the homes, twice as many in frame houses as in tar-paper shacks, had either a crucifix, a statue, or a print of some Saint.

Seven of the frame houses and fourteen of the tar-paper shacks had taxidermic products attached to walls.

In the early day, every man owned one or more bows and many arrows. Food supply, to some extent, depended on the skillful use of them. Defense of lodge and tribe, too, might depend on them. Bows and arrows were replaced by guns with the coming of the fur traders. Today they have completely replaced them, but not all men own guns. Sixty-eight guns—nearly an equal number in both types of houses—were found in the one hundred fifty homes. One family in a tar-paper shack owned six guns.

CONCLUSIONS

In the interior decoration of tar-paper shacks traditional Chippewa art and taxidermic products were found more often than in frame houses. In frame houses, on the contrary, articles of needlecraft, flowers, enlarged photographs, collections of snap shots and religious articles were found more often than in tar-paper shacks.

MUSIC: PHONOGRAPHS, RADIOS, INSTRUMENTS

Musical instruments used by the Chippewa when the white man first met them consisted of several types of drums, of the rattle, and of the flute.

The Midē wiwin drum, a hollowed basswood log covered at one end with heavy tanned deerhide, is still being used during the Midē wiwin ceremonial. Two Midē wiwin drums were found in the one hundred fifty families, one was being used in the ceremonial held at Ponsford in June, 1938, while the other was in the home of its owner, a member of the Leech Lake Midē wiwin. Both owners belonged to the tar-paper shack group.

A drum used in producing the rhythm for social dances, such as the "pow-wows"—a dance given for tourists and for commercial purposes—is made by stretching tanned deerhides over a circular band of an inner layer of basswood twelve inches in width and about three feet in diameter. A man of the tar-paper shack group, an expert in the making of these, was completing one in July, 1938.

One man of the tar-paper shack group, too, had a small drum, such as is used by Midē wiwin members who possess curative or predictive powers. These drums consist of a band of wood, two to three inches in depth and eight inches in diameter. Over both sides of the band, raw untanned hairless deerhide is stretched, the ends of the hide being sewed together with strips of rawhide.

Rattles, consisting of small wooden cylinders covered with tanned hide and containing small stones or shot, are used during the Midē wiwin ceremonial and by the Grand Medicine men whenever they exercise their powers. Four such rattles were being used during the ceremonial at Ponsford, two of these belonging to families living in tar-paper shacks; no information was gotten relative to the other two.

No flutes were found in the group. Flutes, as may be recalled, were used by lovers, in the early day. They were made of softwood, such as ash, cedar, or box elder. They usually had six finger holes.

Twenty-six musical instruments, other than those of Chippewa origin, were found in the families. These ranged from pianos to harmonicas. Two pianos and two organs were found in frame houses while none were found in tar-paper shacks. One of the pianos had belonged to the mother of the present owner; the other was bought by a father for his daughter in the boom days of allotment sales. The two organs were bought for the present owners when they became of age and their allotments were sold. They were the girls' share of their allotments, the remainder of their money being used to help pay family debts or for other purposes. "My father and mother went on a long trip while I stayed home and cared for the children. When they returned they brought me an organ. That's all I ever got out of my allotment!" said one of the owners of an organ.

Guitars were the most prevalent instrument in the group. Six were found in frame houses, three in tar-paper shacks, and one in a rehabilitation house. Other musical instruments found in frame houses were two harmonicas, two ukuleles, one violin, and one banjo. In tar-paper shacks, one harmonica, one accordion, one ukulele, one violin, and two banjos were seen.

Individual musical instruments, it seems, could well play an important part in the recreation and in the occupation of leisure time in the homes. Pianos and organs are out of the question, considering the size of the homes and the subsistence standard of living of the families. To the possession of smaller instruments, however, little objection could be raised. These are comparatively inexpensive, can be easily carried into the open where Indians spend much of their summer time, and to friends' homes or to distant places, if work is found there. Once the curriculum of schools for Indians is based on the actual need, facilities, and interests of Indians, the teaching of the use of small musical instruments might well be included.

Seventy-two, or more than half of the families (forty-six in frame houses, twenty-two in tar-paper shacks, and four in rehabilitation houses), had radios. Fifteen of those in frame houses were still being paid for; so were eleven in tar-paper shacks and one in a rehabilitation house. Of the entire seventy-two, only five, and all of these in frame houses, were operated by means of electricity; all others were operated by batteries. In thirteen frame houses and twelve tar-paper shacks, radios were not in use, since batteries needed recharging. Recharging, as well as trips to towns in which recharging is done, cost a price.

Thirteen of the radios in frame houses, one in a rehabilitation house, and one in a tar-paper shack, were console style. Prices of these varied from $15.00 for second-hand ones to $125.00 for new ones. In a number of instances, old phonographs, old sewing machines, wild rice, etc., had been traded in the purchase of them. Four families in frame houses and three in tar-paper shacks owned phonographs but no radios. Five of these, however, hoped to trade them for radios as soon as they got "a little ahead in payment of other bills."

The radios varied in number of tubes, the five-tube being the mode for the tar-paper shacks (eleven cases) and the six-tube, for the frame houses (fourteen cases). Only two eight-tube radios were found in tar-paper shacks, while eight were seen in frame houses. The Coronado style prevailed in both groups for nine of the twenty-two in tar-paper shacks and twenty of the forty-six in frame houses were of this make. Philco ranked next; and Airline, third.

CONCLUSIONS

The traditional musical instruments were definitely related to housing since all those found in the group were owned by tar-paper shack dwellers. Pianos and organs were owned exclusively by frame-house dwellers. Smaller musical instruments were not related to housing. Radios were related to housing, not only in numbers but also in models, for only one of the fourteen console models was found in a tar-paper shack. The five-tube radio prevailed in tar-paper shacks; the six-tube in frame houses. The Coronado was the favorite style. The number of radios that were still being paid for and the number that needed recharging were not related to housing since nearly an equal number was found in both groups.

RUGS

In the early day, floor mats were woven of bulrushes or of the inner bark of the cedar tree. Bulrushes formed the warp and the inner bark of the basswood tree the woof, in the former; in the cedar mats, both warp and woof were of cedar. If a pattern was desired in the bulrush mats, some of the rushes were dyed, as previously noted. Both types of mats, when new, served largely as tables, being spread out on the ground with food and dishes resting on them. They were rolled and stored near the wall of the wigwam when not in use. Worn mats were used as rugs, the family squatting or resting on them.

Bulrush mats are still being made by Chippewa of the first and second generations on the White Earth Reservation. One old couple of the Round Lake community was pulling bulrushes at Ice-cracking Lake in the summer of 1938. Eight of the seventy-one families living in tar-paper shacks possessed bulrush mats. Some were merely keepsakes, women having received them from mothers or grandmothers, while others were used for squatting purposes in berry patches or while out gathering wild rice, moisture penetrating them less easily than rag rugs.

Rush mats had been replaced in many homes by braided rag rugs and linoleum. Braided rugs of six or eight ply were found in more than half of the families, one family in a frame house having as many as twelve and one in a tar-paper shack as many as ten. Table XX lists the types of rugs found in the families.

TABLE XX

Types of Rugs Found in One Hundred Fifty
Chippewa Indian Families on the White Earth Reservation in 1938

RUGS	TAR-PAPER SHACK FAMILIES	FRAME-HOUSE FAMILIES	U.S. REHABILITATION- HOUSE FAMILIES	ALL ITEMS
Traditional bulrush mats	8	–	–	8
Braided rag rugs of six or eight ply	35	38	6	79
Small factory-woven rugs	3	5	2	10
Large factory-woven rugs	–	7	–	7
Small linoleum rugs	8	10	2	20
Large linoleum rugs	14	26	3	43

CONCLUSIONS

Both types of houses, therefore, used braided rugs, in nearly equal proportion. Of all other types, frame-house dwellers owned more.

READING MATTER IN THE HOMES

The Chippewa in the early days had no written language other than picture writing. Picture writing consisted of crude delineations of men, birds, animals, and other material objects, and of symbolisms that represented sky, earth, lakes, hills, days, directions, and numbers. Old men say that every band had several men well versed in these symbols and signs who, by combining them in ideographs so as to represent progressive action, could send a communication to another Chippewa and make themselves well understood. Most Chippewa could read messages, records of time, directions, or maps designed for travel, but only the initiated could read the records, writings, and songs of the Midē wiwin and those used in working charms.[11] Picture writing was usually done with a pointed bone on the inner surface of birch bark, or on layers of wood of cedar or ash, the figures being filled in with charcoal or colored soil.

Traditionally, then, the Chippewa had no reading matter in their homes. Bishop Baraga, one of the earliest Catholic missionaries among the Chippewa, wrote a grammar and a dictionary of the Chippewa language and also a prayer book, a catechism, and some books of instruction for his people. Copies of these are still extant and were being used by those in the families of this study who could read Chippewa.

Contact with European civilization had either not created a desire for reading in the one hundred fifty families or it had not provided the means and facilities for so doing. Very few homes had any reading material other than newspapers and cheap periodicals. Table XXI denotes the reading matter in the homes.

TABLE XXI

Reading Matter in One Hundred Fifty
Chippewa Indian Families on the White Earth Reservation in 1938

READING MATTER	TAR-PAPER SHACK FAMILIES	FRAME-HOUSE FAMILIES	U.S. REHABILITATION-HOUSE FAMILIES	ALL ITEMS
Reference books or books of fiction	11	17	3	31
Set of encyclopedias	1	1	–	2
Text books	9	7	–	16
Sunday papers regularly purchased	43	45	5	93
Daily papers subscribed for	2	6	2	10
Periodicals subscribed for	12	17	2	31
Periodicals regularly purchased	6	9	–	15

The following are titles of some of the books found in the homes: *Life of Pope Leo XIII, Library of Health, Bunny Brown and His Sister Sue, Red Pepper Burns, Molly Make-Believe, Alice in Wonderland, Strawberry Roan, The Bible, The Girl Scouts of the Open Road, Practical Sewing and Dress Making, Bible Readings for Home Circles, How to Keep Well, The Little Giant Encyclopedia, Beautiful Joe, A Boy's Life of General Pershing, Will Rogers, Indian Wars.*

The usual answer to the question: "What books have you?" was, "Not any." This answer was generally accompanied by a smile, and, occasionally, by a hearty laughter, especially from the older and from the illiterate people. "We don't read any books and our children get plenty of them in school," was another frequent answer. "The Montgomery Ward catalog is the only one" was so frequent a response that the writer regrets not having recorded the number of times it was given. Another recurring reply was, "No one in this house ever reads anything except the 'funnies.' We get the Sunday paper to read those."

In nearly all cases the Sunday papers were bought from "the man that comes by here selling them," evidently a distributor of the Minneapolis *Tribune* and St. Paul *Pioneer Press,* for twenty-three in each group of tar-paper shacks and frame houses and three of the rehabilitation homes bought the Minneapolis *Tribune,* and six in each group of tar-paper shacks and frame houses the St. Paul *Pioneer Press.* Several purchased their Sunday paper at stores in town, "when we go to church." Among the tar-paper shack people doing so, three purchased the Minneapolis *Journal,* five the Chicago *Herald Tribune,* and five the weekly issue of one of the Detroit Lakes papers. Five of the tar-paper shack dwellers and twenty-one of the frame-house people bought two Sunday papers, the "funnies" being the attraction. Of the frame-house people, one bought the Minnesota *Leader;* one, the *Farmer Laborite;* one, *Grit;* seven, the Mahnomen paper; and six, one of the Detroit Lakes papers.

Subscribers for the daily paper were receiving the Minneapolis *Star* and the St. Paul *Pioneer Press.* Most of the thirty-one families who subscribed to some periodical were receiving the *Farmer's Wife,* and the *Farmer;* several had subscribed to St. *Anthony's Messenger, Sacred Heart Messenger* and the *Literary Digest.* Fifteen of the families (nine in frame houses and six in tar-paper shacks) bought periodicals in stores. Inquiries at stores in White Earth village, Ponsford, Mahkoonce Corners, and Daigles Mills—all of them located on the reservation—verified suspicions that *Love and Romance, True Stories, True Romances, True Experiences, True Detective,* and *True Confessions* were the periodicals that were being bought by the Indians. Young people were found reading these in many of the homes. They might as easily have purchased the *Ladies Home Journal, Liberty, Saturday Evening Post, Literary Digest, Cosmopolitan,* or the better periodicals at the same stores for they were being sold there. A few of the Indians did buy the better ones.

There were no library facilities within easy reach of most of the people, Mahnomen being the only town on the reservation having a public library. Since neither homes nor public libraries supplied the families with good, wholesome reading material, it seemed that a circulating library might well have been introduced, either through the Education Division of the U.S. Bureau of Indian Affairs or in co-operation with the Minnesota State Department of Education.

CONCLUSIONS

It was certain that occupants of both tar-paper shacks and frame houses were in need of wholesome reading material; both groups were lacking it. Frame-house dwellers led by six in those who owned library books; by two in those who purchased Sunday papers; by five in those who subscribed for periodicals; and by two in those who purchased them. Tar-paper shack people led by two in the possession of text books.

THE YARD, SUN SHELTERS

If the interiors of most of the homes of the families were unattractive, the yards were decidedly so. They were not only unattractive but were usually littered with broken dishes, rags, discarded clothes, chips of wood, toys, at times the excreta of animals and in some instances, of humans. Only thirty-two of the families (twenty-five in frame houses, three in tar-paper shacks, and four in rehabilitation houses) made definite attempts at having some sort of lawn and of making the yard attractive. Thirty-seven of the families (thirteen in frame houses, seventeen in tar-paper shacks, and seven in rehabilitation houses) had planted flowers. Some planted them because they wished to beautify the surroundings; some, because they loved flowers; others had been given flower seeds along with other seeds and planted them when they planted their gardens. The remaining families made no attempt whatsoever at having a lawn or of even keeping the wild grass cut. Some older Indians whose yards were noticeably well cared for observed that variations in ability to keep homes and surroundings clean and attractive existed in the old days the same as they do today. Fifty-six of the families (thirty-six in frame houses, seventeen in tar-paper shacks, and three in rehabilitation houses) had fences about their yards.

Traditional sun shelters were found in the yards of four of the tar-paper shacks. Sun shelters consist of large branches of trees resting on a raft of poles that is kept elevated at the corners by four saplings five or six feet long sunk well into the ground. In five additional cases (one in a frame house and four in tar-paper shacks) canvas replaced the branches. Sun shelters in traditional days were always erected in open spaces where the wind had free play. The woods near the house might provide shade but no breeze, for the underbrush obstructed the wind.

CONCLUSIONS

The exterior surroundings of most of the homes were unattractive. Fewer than one-fifth of them had lawns and flower beds. More than eight times as many frame-house dwellers as tar-paper shack occupants made the exterior of their homes attractive by caring for lawns; more than twice as many had fences about their yards. Tar-paper shacks led by four in the raising of flowers. Only nine of the families had sun shelters, and eight of these were found near tar-paper shacks.

PRIVATE UTILITIES

DRINKING WATER: SOURCES

In the early days wigwams were located only where there was a supply of water, that is, near a spring, a river, a creek, or a lake. Fresh or clear water was seldom drunk, a decoction being made by boiling water and steeping an herb or root in it. Often wild honey or maple sugar was added to create a pleasant taste. Old Chippewa today tell that they can count the times that they have partaken of clear fresh water.

Fifteen of the one hundred fifty families (three in frame houses and twelve in tar-paper shacks) were using drinking water from flowing springs, and one in each group was drinking river water. In no case was it being boiled except where old people were drinking decoctions, "letting it boil a little and then brewing it on the stove for hours." The remaining families were drawing their drinking water from wells. All families, except a few living in isolated areas, were using community wells or wells dug at public expense for several families in the vicinity. In all but a few cases the families had to carry or haul their water. If conditions of ill health or occupation prevented members of a family from fetching it, water was bought from a water peddler.

One wonders how the families under these conditions—most of them carrying water some distances or buying it—could meet a standard considered a fundamental need by the Committee on the Hygiene of

Housing. The committee notes that "Cleanliness of the dwelling depends in part on such construction as will facilitate cleansing; both dwelling cleanliness and personal cleanliness demand an ample supply of water (twenty gallons per capita per day as a minimum for household use), with facilities for heating water. The ends in view are justified in part by the role of clean hands in preventing the spread of germ diseases, but on an even wider base they may be considered essential to self respect from a psychological standpoint."[12]

CONCLUSIONS

It is difficult to infer whether there is any relationship between housing and water supply, since individually owned wells were practically entirely lacking in both tar-paper shack and frame-house groups. It is true, however, that more tar-paper shack people used spring water than did frame-house dwellers. Spring water was being used largely by people living in isolated places, but it so happened that those living in isolated places generally lived in tar-paper shacks.

TOILET FACILITIES

The use of privies is not a part of the traditional culture of the Chippewa any more than it is of most primitive tribes. When the area about the camps became filthy with garbage, refuse, and excreta, the camp was moved to a clean place—land and groves were plentiful.

Fourteen of the families (eleven in tar-paper shacks and three in frame houses) were without privies. Ten of these families lived in isolation, and four lived close enough together to form a group. Fifteen of the families (nine in tar-paper shacks and six in frame houses) had privies constructed of half a dozen or more wide planks raised in an erect position around a seat. These provided at least some privacy. All of the rehabilitation houses had well-constructed sanitary outdoor toilets. Most of the privies, excepting those belonging to the rehabilitation homes, were badly in need of repair and of transfer. None of the families had indoor toilets.

CONCLUSIONS

The lack of privies and the need of better ones was more closely related to tar-paper shacks than to frame houses.

ECONOMIC RESOURCES

INCOME

Money was not a part of the old Chippewa culture pattern, each family being an economically self-sufficing unit. And rarely, in the old days, was anyone under obligations, economically, to anyone else. Neighborliness, kindness, and sharing were the order of the day. To get an exact equivalent was considered beneath his dignity by a Chippewa.

If a family had more than it needed to supply its wants, it made gifts of the superfluous. Gifts might be made, however, with an eye on a return gift. The proper etiquette for so doing is exemplified in an event told by an old woman. She had made a very fine birch-bark waste basket and brought it to a white woman, who, she knew, had received discarded clothes which were to be distributed to the Indians. (She herself needed a warm coat.) She brought the basket in the forenoon of a day and gave it to the white woman as a gift; in the afternoon, she returned to ask for the coat. She had merely followed tribal etiquette. Tribal etiquette, however, is not always understood as proper etiquette by whites. A visiting Indian woman who was present when the above story was told asked: "Weren't you told, 'Oh, yes! That's just what I expected! That's the way the Indians do, sly around and pretend to do you a favor, but all the while they are planning something!' I was told that once. But that's the way it's all through; those whites don't understand us and we never seem to know what they're after!"

With the coming of the white man trade began. Furs and canoes were exchanged for broadcloth, blankets, shawls, kettles, glass beads, firearms, and "firewater." Barter was the method of exchange for a long time; it was material goods, not coins, that the Indians wanted and needed. Old Chippewa on the White Earth Reservation today tell that it was not until the sale of allotments and timber rights that many of the Indians possessed money.

The days of allotment and timber sales date back to 1904. Many Chippewa had large sums of money at that time and might have deposited them at interest. But, since storing the superfluous was never a part of their culture–the Chippewa were sharers–banking money was not done by them. Saving money is not part of the Chippewa tribal background.

The income of most of the White Earth Indians today maintains them only on a subsistence standard of living, and it is, therefore, impossible for them to save any money, should saving money have become part of their culture pattern. Only one of the families of this study had money deposited in a bank. And only two men and one woman, all three living in frame houses, had life insurance.

When this study was begun it was intended that income and expenditure of the families be included. Early in the preliminary survey it was discovered, however, that income could be determined rather quickly and to a large extent accurately since most of it came from relief projects, but that it would be practically impossible to determine expenditures and to obtain reliable information regarding them. Selling liquor to an Indian is unlawful, but drinking is one of the greatest evils on the reservation and much money is spent on it. Because of this difficulty, it was decided to include only income in so far as it could be accurately determined.

Of the one hundred fifty families, one hundred forty-eight were drawing U.S. Government checks of either W.P.A., C.C.C.-I.D., World War veterans' pensions, Social Security Act, or I.S. Division of Roads' funds. One family only was self-supporting, having a cash income of an average of $55.00 a month from the sale of cream; another family was on direct relief.

The following table indicates the source of income of the families, as well as the type and number of unpaid bills.

TABLE XXII

Some Phases of Economic Life of One Hundred Fifty
Chippewa Indian Families on the White Earth Reservation in 1938

INCOME AND UNPAID BILLS	TAR-PAPER SHACK FAMILIES	FRAME-HOUSE FAMILIES	U.S. REHABILITATION- HOUSE FAMILIES	ALL ITEMS
Income				
Families drawing U.S.				
Government checks	70	70	8	148
W.P.A	46	48	8	102
C.C.C.-I.D.	9	3	–	12
I.S. Division of Roads	–	5	–	5
Pensions–World				
War veterans	2	1	–	3
Pensions–Widows of				
World War veterans	2	2	–	4
Social Security Act				
(& State of Minnesota)				
Old age assistance				
(persons)	23	9	1	33

TABLE XXII *(continued)*

INCOME AND UNPAID BILLS	TAR-PAPER SHACK FAMILIES	FRAME-HOUSE FAMILIES	U.S. REHABILITATION-HOUSE FAMILIES	ALL ITEMS
Income				
Direct county relief	1	–	–	1
Self-supporting (dairying)	–	1	–	1
Unpaid bills				
Grocery	41	42	7	90
Clothing	3	7	–	10
Automobiles, pickups, trucks	13	16	–	29
Stoves	3	12	2	17
Radios	11	15	2	28
Sewing machines	1	2	–	3
Washing machines	6	8	2	16
Other bills	12	12	2	26

W.P.A. projects, as may be recalled, were located at White Earth village and at Ponsford. One person in 102 of the families, either husband, wife, son or daughter, was employed on W.P.A. jobs. Eighty-seven of these were men (forty-one from frame houses, forty from tar-paper shacks, and six from rehabilitation houses) while fifteen were women (seven from frame houses, six from tar-paper shacks, and two from rehabilitation houses).

The C.C.C.-I.D. was located at Naytahwaush and employed only men. Five men of the frame-house group, four living in White Earth and one in Waubun, were employed by I.S. Division of Roads.

Three disabled World War veterans and four widows of World War veterans who were killed in action were receiving pensions. The Social Security Act, as administered in the State of Minnesota, includes Indians. Thirty-three Indians of the families received old age assistance. Fifteen of these were widowed persons; eighteen were couples. Two of the couples lived in frame houses, and seven in tar-paper shacks. Of the widowed persons, five lived in frame houses, nine in tar-paper shacks, and one in a rehabilitation house. One of the families in a tar-paper shack was on direct relief, both parents being unable to work.

Cash income approximated the following: W.P.A. checks amounted to $44.00 a month in the case of the ordinary worker; to $60.00 for supervisors; and to $77.00 if the worker used his own truck. The checks for the C.C.C.–I.D. amounted to $45.00 per month. The men employed on the I.S. roads received $88.00 a month, one receiving $155.00. The amounts received from the U.S. Veteran's Bureau varied, the lowest being $42.00, the highest $66.00. Old age assistance, too, varied from $20.00 to $43.00 for a couple and from $15.00 to $20.00 for a widowed person. The income in twelve of the homes (nine frame houses and three tar-paper shacks) was increased by the earnings of boys at C.C.C.

Many parents complained that their income was insufficient; that it paid for food but not for clothing. That $44.00 was insufficient for a family of four to eight or more persons was true; but it was difficult to understand why some parents having so meager an income felt that it was their privilege to spend any of it on liquor, as not a small number did. Many, too, might have saved from their income for clothes by cultivating gardens sufficiently large for immediate, as well as for storage, use.

In a few homes, income was increased by special effort. One physically disabled woman who lived with her daughter supported herself by the sale of beadwork; another cleaned houses at sixty cents an hour; one sewed. Two men took odd jobs at summer resorts, when not busy on W.P.A.; two did farm work.

Many of the families had to meet unpaid bills each pay day. Inability on the part of adults to budget their income and expenditures seemed to occur in most of the families. To live on a budget would have seemed to be an easy matter, since cash income was a definite, bi-weekly amount and the amount needed for groceries could be determined, at least approximately, for groceries had been bought on credit and paid for every pay day for several years past. Illustrations showing inability to plan expenditures advantageously could have been found in many families. Several follow: A thirty-one-year-old son, the sole support of his mother and five brothers and sisters, after being employed on W.P.A. for only three months, bought a $350.00 car, making $10.00 monthly payments on it. His mother was proud of the car and wanted us to see it. "When we have paid for it, we'll buy a radio," she remarked. Neither she nor her son had calculated that it would require nearly three years to pay for the car.

A fifty-two-year-old woman showed us her household equipment with much pride. Two years ago she had bought a sewing-machine for $105.00 from a salesman from Bemidji; she still owed him $33.00. Five months previous to our visit she had bought a fine, new stove for $63.00 from an agent from Mahnomen; she had paid all but $34.00 on it. A month before she had bought a gasoline washing machine worth $116.00, the salesman, however, allowing her $90.00 for her old machine; she had $20.00 to pay on it still. "We are having a little hard time now paying all the bills," she remarked. "But I meet all the payments as they come due, and let the grocery bills wait. I can't be expected to pay everything at once; my old man only earns $45.00 in C.C.C.–I.D."

Automobiles, pickups, or trucks, listed among unpaid bills, were being paid for on the installment plan. In all cases they were second-hand cars ranging in cost from $15.00 to $110.00. Twenty-six families were paying bills, such as physician's, renting of cars for trips, etc.

CONCLUSIONS

It was difficult to relate cash income to housing since the relief projects were located in certain communities and workers for them were drawn from the local people. But communities were distinguishable by the types of houses found in them for such villages as Naytahwaush, Ponsford, and Beaulieu had a large number of tar-paper shacks while those of White Earth village, Waubun, Callaway, and Bijou had more frame houses.

Old age assistance, however, could be compared, since it was granted indiscriminately to all persons over sixty-five years of age. The number of couples receiving old age pensions living in tar-paper shacks exceeded those in frame houses by five, while the widowed ones did by three.

No relationship existed between housing and unpaid bills for groceries. Frame houses, however, exceeded tar-paper shacks by four in unpaid bills for clothing; by three in automobiles and trucks; by nine in stoves; by two in washmachines; and by four in radios. Tar-paper shacks exceeded frame houses by one in unpaid sewing machines.

GARDENING AND CANNING FOODS

Traditionally, gardening consisted of cultivating small plots of ground scattered haphazardly among the tall grass in spaces exposed to the sun. These patches were generally near the winter camp which, as may be recalled, was usually located in maple groves. Corn, squash, pumpkin, and beans were planted in them during the maple-sugar-making season, and the plot was hoed and cared for until it was time to move into the berry patches. At the end of the wild-rice season, the families returned to gather their harvest. Corn on the cobs was braided by the husks, thus allowing the kernels to dry. Pumpkins and squash were cut in circular fashion beginning at the stem end; the long strips being dried in the sun while hanging across elevated poles made of saplings. Garden plots of the traditional type were seen on the Red Lake and the Lac du Flambeau reservations in the summers of 1932 and 1935.

The raising of vegetables was, therefore, part of the Chippewa culture pattern. Some Chippewa of the one hundred fifty families had flourishing gardens while the gardens of others were conspicuous in their scantiness, often made more so because several rods away some Indians or whites had grown luxuriant ones. All but nineteen of the families (ten in tar-paper shacks, eight in frame houses, and one in a rehabilitation house) had gardens. Many of them contained squash, pumpkin, corn, potatoes, beets, carrots, onions, rutabaga, turnips, and cabbage.

It was difficult to obtain the size of the gardens or even to estimate them with any accuracy. They not only consisted of irregular patches and of all sizes but some families had planted several gardens, one near the home and others at some distance. Even the cost of plowing did not indicate the size, for costs varied in different communities. Some, too, plowed their own or had relatives do it gratis. Those who paid were charged varying prices ranging from 75¢ to $5.00.

It is significant, however, that of all families who had planted gardens only sixty per cent or ninety in number (forty-one in tar-paper shacks, forty-three in frame houses, and six in rehabilitation houses) had had in mind storing or preserving some of the vegetables for winter use. In connection with this, it is interesting to note, too, that twenty-eight per cent or forty-three of the families (twenty-eight in tar-paper shacks and fifteen in frame houses) had done no canning of food in the fall of 1937. If we add to these, the forty families (eighteen in tar-paper shacks, seventeen in frame houses and five in rehabilitation houses), who canned fewer than fifty quarts in the same fall, we have fifty-five per cent who benefited little from their gardens for winter supply except for potatoes and dried beans.

The inability of some to buy Mason jars may have been one factor in the small amount of canning that was done. One couple, however, would not consider canning any food. "Too many people get poisoned from canned foods," the father remarked. Thirty-one families, or twenty per cent of the entire group (twelve living in tar-paper shacks, seventeen in frame houses, and two in rehabilitation houses) canned from two hundred to five hundred quarts each; one in a frame house had canned six hundred quarts.

It was difficult to understand why more families did not raise fruit trees and berries. Both grow well in the area and of neither is there any longer a wild or uncultivated supply, forest fires having ruined the area repeatedly. Only nine families (three in tar-paper shacks, five in frame houses, and one in a rehabilitation house) had berries in their gardens.

CONCLUSIONS

It is evident that there is little relationship between housing and the number of gardens planted, for tar-paper shack dwellers exceeded those in frame houses only by two, while the exact reverse was true in the storing of garden vegetables for winter use. The neglect in raising fruit trees and berries was equally conspicuous in both groups.

In the canning of food, however, there appeared to be a definite relationship. The mean number of quarts canned in the fall of 1937 for tar-paper shack people was seventy; for frame-house dwellers, 105; and for rehabilitation-house occupants, 118. Tar-paper shack dwellers, therefore, canned from thirty to forty-eight fewer quarts than did the others. It is possible, however, that the latter dried corn and beans for winter, according to the old way. Furthermore, tar-paper shack people exceeded the frame-house group by thirteen in those who did no canning.

DOMESTICATED ANIMALS

Traditionally, a variety of breeds of dogs were the only domesticated animals the Chippewa had. Today, domesticated animals, other than dogs and cats, are still conspicuously absent from their environment. Eighty-five of the families (thirty-seven in tar-paper shacks, forty-two in frame houses, and six in rehabilitation houses) had one or more dogs; fifteen of them had two, nine of these families living in tar-paper shacks. In cases where there were two dogs, one was usually a hunting dog while the other was a pet. One might have expected a cat in every home, since mice and rats had easy access to most of them. But only seventy-nine of the homes (thirty-nine frame houses, thirty-five tar-paper shacks, and five rehabilitation houses) had cats.

Apparently chickens could be raised on the reservation by most families if they had the will or the enthusiasm to do so. Only sixteen of the families, however, (nine living in frame houses, five in tar-paper shacks, and two in rehabilitation houses) had chickens. One of the reasons for not raising them was that wire fences which were required to keep the chickens from getting into their own and neighbor's gardens were costly. This was undoubtedly true, but in a number of instances better budgeting of the income would have provided some fencing, at least. Furthermore, the families who were raising chickens lived in the villages largely and they had provided themselves with fences. Five of these were located in frame houses in White Earth village with an average of thirty-one chickens per family, and two in rehabilitation houses with an average of fourteen each. Five families in tar-paper shacks in Ponsford had an average of nine each; one family in Beaulieu had nine. One family in the open country, in the Rice Lake area, had twenty-eight chickens; another, at Round Lake had four. Others found it difficult to house and to maintain chickens through the winter. There is, undoubtedly, some truth in this for tar-paper coops would not protect chickens from the cold, and, as to maintenance, families often found it difficult to supply themselves with food and clothing during the winter months. Families who did keep several chickens through the winter usually took them into their homes.

It would seem, however, that chicks could be purchased in the spring, raised during the summer, and either eaten or cold-packed in the fall. Only nineteen of the one hundred fifty families (eight in each group of tar-paper shacks and frame houses, and three in rehabilitation houses) had purchased chicks in the spring of 1938, the price being ten cents or less a piece. The average number purchased by frame-house people was forty-four; by tar-paper shack people, twenty-nine; by rehabilitation-house dwellers, thirty-three. The mortality among chicks was large since most of the families had no coops, rain and cold killing many. Possibly the reply of one man, to the remark that we were confused over the lack of interest by the Chippewa on so many reservations in the raising of chickens since fowl formed an important part of the diet in the early days, is of some value: "We don't like tame fowl very much. A chicken doesn't taste like wild duck any more than beef tastes like venison!"

Cows, too, were not owned by most of the families; eighteen of the families (eight in each of the frame-house and tar-paper shack groups, and two in the rehabilitation houses) owned a total of thirty-four. Three of the tar-paper shack families and six of the frame-house people owned calves.

Not being farmers these people had no need for horses. Three families owned a team of horses and were using them mostly on government road projects; three others owned one horse each. Four of the owners of horses lived in frame houses and two in tar-paper shacks. One family in a tar-paper shack owned two sheep; another, a pig; and one, a canary bird.

CONCLUSIONS

The possession of domesticated animals was noticeably not a part of the environment of the one hundred fifty families. Families were not interested in raising domesticated animals nor were the latter considered an economic asset. Families did not have the wherewith to provide shelter for them and, in the case of large animals, water supply was an added problem since it was usually located at some distance. There was practically no relationship between the possession of domesticated animals and housing. Frame houses led by five in the number possessing dogs; by nine for cats; and by two for horses. Both groups had an equal number of families interested in raising chicks and cows.

PROVIDING FOOD OF THE CHIPPEWA PATTERN: WILD RICE,
MAPLE SUGAR, DRIED FISH AND MEAT

Wild rice, maple sugar, dried fish and meat formed part of the traditional menu of the Chippewa. Wild rice, maple sap, fish, and wild game were plentiful in the Chippewa country in the early day and could be taken unhampered. Today, Minnesota game laws apply to the White Earth Indians as they do to all citizens of the state, and therefore fishing and hunting adds to their food only in a small degree. Many of the maple groves belong to whites, and whites are not always willing to allow tapping of trees. It is expected, however, that wild rice may soon be revived as a staple food.

Wild rice is an annual plant which grows in lakes and slow moving streams of mud bottoms. It is gathered in late August and early September. The U.S. Department of Agriculture, the Minnesota State Forestry, the University of Minnesota, the Minnesota State Conservation Commission, and the Chippewa National Forest Commission are all interested in a study that is now under way for conservation and production of wild rice. It is hoped that by proper methods of conservation and by advantageous means of marketing it, the annual income of the Indians will be increased by the harvesting and sale of it.

Wild rice is found along the shores of several of the lakes on the White Earth Reservation, especially on those of Rice Lake. The rice, however, was practically drowned out in these lakes in the spring of 1938 due to high waters. Consequently, families from the White Earth Reservation who wished to gather wild rice in the fall went to Star Lake near Perham, Minnesota, or to Height-of-land Lakes near Park Rapids, Minnesota. Figures telling the number of families who had gathered wild rice in the fall of 1938 were not available when this study was being completed. In the fall of 1937, however, forty-three of the families (eight in frame houses and thirty-five in tar-paper shacks) had gathered rice. All of them used some for home consumption and thirty-one (twenty-seven in frame houses and four in tar-paper shacks) sold some.

In the fall of 1938, green, or unparched rice, was selling at the camps along the lakes for ten cents a pound; good grades of parched rice, for forty cents a pound. Several of the women harvested as many as one hundred pounds of green rice in a day.

Maple sugar is made early in the spring of the year, maple trees being tapped for sap. In the early days each family of Chippewa had a portion of trees in a maple grove known to it as its sugar bush. If its permanent lodge was not located in a maple grove, it moved into its sugar bush and erected there some wigwams—usually one for the family, one for the boiling of the sap, and one for storing the needed utensils. All this done, the trees were tapped by very primitive methods—which methods still prevail—the sap boiled, evaporated, and refined.

Many of the first- and second-generation Indians of the one hundred fifty families complained that the limited number of maple groves on the reservation were owned by white people and that these objected to the trees being tapped. Only seven of the families (two in frame houses and five in tar-paper shacks) made maple sugar in the spring of 1938; one of the frame-house dwellers and two of the tar-paper shack people sold some.

Salting down meat and fish, or cold-packing them, was unknown to the early Chippewa. They preserved fish and meat by drying and, incidentally, smoking them over a slow fire. The backs of the fish were slit so that the entire framework of bone could be removed, then, with belly up, they were placed astride bars which rested on crotched sticks, or they were placed in the crotch of an inclined stick leaning over the fire. If many fish were to be dried, a rack consisting of cross bars of saplings, the corner of the rack resting on crotched sticks two feet or less from the ground, was placed over a fire. All of the above methods were in use on Chippewa reservations within recent years.

The families of this study did little fishing except for immediate use. This may be largely due to a state law which limits the number of fish per person per day to ten. The older Chippewa find it difficult to understand that such a law should be applied to Indians and most of them give little heed to it. A seventy-year-old woman of one of the families was busily engaged, one of the days we visited her, in fastening the traditional cedar floaters and the stone sinkers to her net. The sun was in the last quarter of its day and she must hurry to set her net. "Nets are set at sunset and are taken in at sunrise," she remarked. She expected a good catch and hoped to dry some; her rack for drying was already prepared.

An old man was caught by the game warden one day with eighteen fish and reminded that ten was the limit for a day. Promptly the old man replied, "Well, I go right back and get us two more and then my old woman and I have ten for today and ten for tomorrow!" Fifteen of the families (three in frame houses and twelve in tar-paper shacks) dried fish whenever possible, using the old method.

Meat, after being cut into long strips, was dried in exactly the same manner as fish. A woman, thirty-two years of age, asked us to trail her along a new path some distance into the woods to see the rack on which she had dried the venison we had seen in her home. In a remote spot in the woods she had cleared a small space of underbrush and erected a rack in the old fashioned manner. She had split branches of trees into slabs and by means of basswood fiber had tied them into a framework. The corners of the framework were resting in the crotches of four saplings about two feet from the ground. Her reason for having the rack deep in the woods was to hide it from the white men. "They take us to court for shooting deer. I was worried that they might see the smoke. Some of them are simply laying for Indians!"

Fourteen of the one hundred fifty families (three in frame houses and eleven in tar-paper shacks) dried meat in the old way. Four families living in frame houses preserved meat for future use by smoking it in modern ways. One smoked it in a smoke-house, another under a large box; one used smoke salt, another liquid smoke.

CONCLUSIONS

Only a few of the families used traditional ways of preserving food. Of those who did, tar-paper shack people led by twenty-seven in wild-rice gathering; by three in the making of maple sugar; by nine in the drying of fish; and by eight in the drying of meat.

SOURCES

1. *A Housing Program for the United States, A Report Prepared for the National Association of Housing Officials* (Chicago: Public Administration Service, 1935), p. 19.
2. "Basic Principles of Healthful Housing." *American Journal of Public Health,* 28:357, March, 1938.
3. *Op. cit.,* p. 354.
4. *Op. cit.,* p. 361.
5. *Op. cit.,* p. 20.

6. *Op. cit.*, p. 360.
7. *Op. cit.*, p. 368.
8. Sister M. Inez Hilger, "Some Phases of Chippewa Material Culture," *Anthropos*, 32 (1937): 782.
9. Frances Densmore, *Chippewa Customs* (U.S. Bureau of American Ethnology Bulletin 86 [1929]), p. 23.
10. Sister M. Inez Hilger, "Chippewa Interpretation of Natural Phenomena," *Scientific Monthly*, 45:179, August, 1937.
11. Sister M. Inez Hilger, "In the Early Days of Wisconsin, An Amalgamation of Chippewa and European Cultures," *Wisconsin Archeologist*, 16:45, June, 1936. Hilger, *Scientific Monthly*, 45:178; Copway, *op. cit.*, p. 131–134.
12. *Op. cit.*, p. 364.

Conclusions

The purpose of this study was to discover whether any social significance existed in the relationship between housing and living conditions and one hundred fifty Chippewa families on the White Earth Reservation of Minnesota. Objectives of the study were expressed in three questions. What are the housing conditions of these Chippewa families? Is there any relationship between the types of houses occupied by them and their aspirations, social problems, and spiritual expressions? Is there any relationship between their housing and their living conditions? The conclusions which follow, it is hoped, are answers to these questions.

HOUSING CONDITIONS

The families were found to be living in houses that could readily be grouped as tar-paper shacks, frame houses, and rehabilitation houses. The last, however, were hardly representative of housing among the Chippewa, for only 3.6 per cent of the families on the White Earth Reservation resided in them.

Tar-paper shacks were clearly indicative of a transition from wigwam to homes built on the American plan. Briefly, a tar-paper shack, as found on the White Earth Reservation, may be defined as a one-story dwelling which consisted of a framework of studding whose walls and low-pitched roof were covered exteriorily with rough boards over which tar paper was tacked, and whose interior walls and ceiling were either unfinished or were covered with rosin paper. The walls ordinarily were eight feet high.* The shack had neither foundation nor porch; its chimney was a stove pipe. There were equal chances that the door at its entrance be homemade or factory-made; that it have a screen door or be without one. Its windows were of any conceivable size or shape, one in every six shacks having broken ones. Four of every five windows were screened. None of the woodwork was painted. There were equal chances that the

*All summaries and percentages in the conclusions are approximations.

shack would consist of one or more than one room, but in no case of more than four. The price of constructing a one-room shack was $27.86; its annual repair was from $6.50 to $7.50. Air space in cubic feet might range from 630 to 5940; if it conformed to the mean for all shacks, it contained 8.07 cubic feet of air space per person per room.

A frame house, as found on the White Earth Reservation, may be defined as a framework of studding with exterior walls and pitched roof covered with rough boards, the boards of the walls being covered with siding and those of the roof with either shingles or tar paper, but more often with the former. The interior walls and ceiling of half the homes were covered with rosin paper and of one-fourth, with lumber; one-tenth were unfinished. The modal height of walls was eight feet. There were equal chances of its having, or not having, a foundation, a porch, and an upstairs. Its doors were generally factory-made and three of every four entrances were screened. One of every three houses had broken windows; all windows were screened. Chimneys were more often of brick than of stove pipe. Three of every five homes consisted of two or three rooms; two of every five had four or more rooms. Both the exterior and the interior of the building were badly in need of paint. Air space in cubic feet ranged from 720 to 10,864. The average number of cubic feet of air space per person per room was 4.17.

A rehabilitation house may be defined as a one- or two-story framework of studding with exterior walls of rough boards overlaid with freshly painted siding. It had a shingled roof, cement foundation, roofed porch, and brick chimney. Interior walls were covered with vertical sheathing. The ceiling was of pressboard. Both walls and ceiling were painted in green and gray. All doors were panelled and all entrances and windows screened; none of the windows was broken. A house might consist of two, three, or four rooms. Air space in cubic feet ranged from 2880 to 5040; if a house conformed in air space to the mean for all rehabilitation houses included in the study, it contained 35.12 cubic feet of air space per person per room.

LIVING CONDITIONS

Housing conditions, then, except for the rehabilitation group, spelt poverty and inadequacy. So did living conditions. But living conditions were closely allied to aspirations, social problems, and spiritual expressions of families, and both were related, in some essential, to housing. Both types of homes–rehabilitation houses being excluded since, as noted before, they were not typical of the housing and living conditions of the families—were overcrowded, lacked living-rooms, had an insufficient number of sleeping-rooms, and needed privacy for both parents and children.

There is no doubt that the above conditions, namely a lack of privacy in sleeping accommodations for both parents and children and the inability of studying and of spending leisure and recreational hours in a suitable place in the home, were important factors in the problems of adults and youths and in the formation of proper ideals and standards in children and adolescents. In former years, the Chippewa child and youth sat by and listened in, and for such silent participants the space of the wigwam was probably sufficient. It is not so with the Chippewa of the third generation of today. The small child in the homes of this study was as noisy and as playful as American children are. He irritated his elders by his boisterous conduct and his mischievousness. However, a Chippewa parent will seldom reprimand or punish a child. Consequently, the child, although corrected, usually does not obey. Habits of disobedience are thereby established and there was evidence in the families that these had been carried into adolescence. Furthermore, if home tasks were assigned to school children, and they undoubtedly were to the upper grades and the high-school groups, where were the children of these homes expected to find isolation and quiet needed for concentration?

The adolescent youth, moreover, not finding accommodations in his home to entertain his friends, especially those of the opposite sex, sought places of more spacious accommodations or of some privacy. He found these not in other homes, for few were less crowded than his own, but in the recreational centers of his community, namely in beer parlors and road houses, in parked automobiles or in strolls on highways, streets, or by-paths. His parents were alarmed at his conduct and late hours, but he had not learnt to obey as a child and saw no need for it now when the importance and independence of youth were upon him.

In another essential, namely that of warm bedding, both groups were nearly equally inadequately supplied. In less essential elements the two groups, also, showed similarities, for nearly an equal number in each group had mantel or alarm clocks, homemade braided rugs, guns, a Sunday paper, and garden flowers.

In other respects, however, decided variations occurred. Living conditions in tar-paper shacks gave evidence of retention of traditional Chippewa culture, of adherence to more primitive ways of living, and of attempts at self-help and self-support. Frame houses came closer to the American standard of living.

Midē wiwin drums and rattles, "pow-wow" drums, bulrush mats, birch-bark baskets and containers were found only in tar-paper shacks. More tar-paper shack dwellers, too, built sun shelters, cooked out-of-doors, tanned deer hides, and gathered medicinal herbs and roots.

Tar-paper shack people showed a greater adherence to primitive ways of living than did frame-house occupants. A larger number of them were without sheets and pillow slips; slept on floors; lacked table cloths and five essential kitchen utensils; were without privies; drank flowing spring water; and cared less for cleanliness and order in their homes.

Tar-paper shack people, too, showed greater efforts at self-help and self-support than did frame-house dwellers. They had more homemade tables and homemade benches; a larger number gathered their own wood, harvested wild rice, made maple sugar, dried fish and meat. They were the only ones who built "oil-drum" heaters. Although they had an income equivalent to that of frame-house people—for both were employed in nearly equal numbers on government relief jobs—they refrained from running bills to the extent that frame-house people did. They had fewer unpaid bills for clothing, radios, automobiles or trucks, stoves, and washing machines.

The frame-house group followed the American standard of living more closely than did the tar-paper shack people. They had a larger number of factory-made tables; of rockers and armchairs; of washing machines; of interior decoration of flowers and needlecraft; of musical instruments of the larger type; of radios; and of storage space, such as cellars and inbuilt closets. They bought fuel to a larger extent and ran bills more readily. They took greater pride in the immediate surroundings of their homes by caring for lawns.

To sum up: The living conditions of the tar-paper shack people indicated clearly that this group was in transition from Chippewa to American standards: They were less well-equipped in both number and kinds of household equipment than were the frame-house dwellers; they had retained a larger number of traits of the old Chippewa material culture; they lived in more primitive ways; and they made greater attempts at self-help and self-support—two virtues that played an important role in the Chippewa culture pattern.

THE FAMILIES

The living conditions of the frame-house families indicated that they were somewhat better equipped than tar-paper shacks in both number and kind of equipment; that their homes were somewhat more attractively arranged; that a larger number of them were cleaner and more orderly; and that the immediate exterior surroundings of their houses were better kept.

Since there was a difference in the living conditions of the families in the two types of houses, one wondered what factors were involved. This study probably does not reveal the multiple factors implicated, but it does indicate that several were operative and that others were obviously not.

Factors not involved, since there was no appreciable difference found in the families of the two groups, were: cash income; the number of children in the family; the total number of occupants of the homes; any unusual differences in the ages of the parents; boarding-school education; birth on or off the reservation; drinking to excess; providing food by means of gardens; or the raising of chickens or cows.

Factors which seemed clearly indicated as functioning, since there was an appreciable difference between the two groups—the difference being in favor of the frame-house group—were: experience off the reservation; education of parents beyond the elementary grades; and membership in the various generations. Living conditions of parents who had had social contacts with persons other than reservation-born and reservation-bred, or who had been exposed to mental stimulation and advantages of educational training beyond the elementary grades, seemed more wholesome, more attractive, and more intelligent than did those who had not had these experiences.

Members of the first generation lived under more primitive conditions than did those of the second and third generation; the second generation gave evidence of a crossing of cultures, while the third lived largely according to American standards. A further difference between the two groups was found in values which centered around home ownership, unpaid bills, and morals. Tar-paper shack occupants prized the ownership of their homes and were less willing to leave them—even for the occupancy of a rehabilitation house—than were frame-house dwellers. They were less prone to having unpaid bills and to buying things on the installment plan, than were frame-house dwellers. Economically, therefore, the tar-paper shack group seemed on a sounder footing than did the frame-house group.

In the field of morals, the study revealed that common-law marriages occurred in the tar-paper shack group many more times than in the frame-house group. Tar-paper shack couples were more apt to separate and enter into common-law marriages, while frame-house couples obtained legal divorces and remarried with ceremony. More than twice as many unmarried mothers were found in frame houses than in tar-paper shacks.

To sum up: Not only had the people of the tar-paper shack group shown transition from wigwam and its life to American standards in housing and living conditions, but they had also shown this transition in their own aspirations and in their interpretation of life: They showed greater cohesion to their own native group than to the whites; they had submitted to less formal education of the American type than had the frame-house people; they preferred to be the owners of their own shacks than to be renters of frame houses or debtors to the United States Government for rehabilitation houses; and they entered into common-law marriages.

FINAL CONCLUSION AND RECOMMENDATIONS

The final conclusion, with several recommendations, is that the one hundred fifty families covered in this survey were, for the most part, a poverty-stricken group who lived in inadequate houses and in an inadequate environment. There is no doubt in the writer's mind that some of the families in both groups were contented to live as they did, and that efforts to assist them or to teach them to assist themselves, would be futile. The factors operative are probably largely psychological. This group is not interested in bettering its housing and living conditions; its members lack both initiative and self-exertion. They are contented to live on a subsistence standard and do not worry about the future; they are convinced that the government will care for them in distress in the future as it has done in the past. There is, on the other hand, a larger group, members of which will undoubtedly profit by any assistance given them, who are anxious and willing to be shown how they may assist themselves. Their experience has been limited and they need to have patient, sympathetic, and helpful teachers. The writer believes that the housing condition of this group should be improved, but that a building program should very definitely solicit the interest and the responsibility of fathers and mothers and older members of the families. Members must be made to feel their importance and their duty in the constructing or rebuilding of their own homes; training them in their responsibilities must be a major part of the rehabilitation program.

It appeared to the writer, too, that several things might well be done to improve the living conditions of this portion of the two groups. Women, trained in homemaking, might be added to the staffs of the extension division on the reservation and to the schools to which girls from these homes are sent for their education—both day and resident schools. The homemaker associated with the extension division could assist mothers and adolescent girls in improving living conditions by instructions in their own homes, by arousing interest, and by assistance in budgeting incomes. The homemakers associated with the schools, on the other hand, might train the future mothers of the reservation in the arts that contribute to finer and better living conditions.

As may be recalled, the two factors that seemed involved in better living conditions were educational advantages beyond elementary grades and experience off the reservation. In order to bring both of these experiences into the lives of the youths of the reservation—future parents of Chippewa homes—the writer would again emphasize the assignment of a liaison person who would give to these youths encouragement, advice, and direction, and whose wisdom and guidance would follow them into the localities in which they may be seeking that experience which is to give them the ability—once grown to manhood and womanhood—of constructing and of enjoying an enriched and comforting environment.

Appendixes

A. Schedule used in the study of housing and living conditions of one hundred fifty Chippewa Indian families on the White Earth Reservation in 1938

B. Maps of the White Earth Reservation and of the Minnesota Chippewa reservations.

C. Summary tabulations of housing conditions of one hundred fifty Chippewa Indian families on the White Earth Reservation of Minnesota in 1938.

D. Summary tabulations descriptive of one hundred fifty Chippewa Indian families on the White Earth Reservation of Minnesota in 1938.

E. Summary tabulations of living conditions of one hundred fifty Chippewa Indian families on the White Earth Reservation of Minnesota in 1938.

F. Illustrations showing housing conditions of one hundred fifty Chippewa Indian families on the White Earth Reservation of Minnesota in 1938.

Appendix A

Indian community   Name–Father

                                                         Mother (maiden)

I. HOUSING CONDITIONS

TYPE OF HOUSE	FOUNDATION	CHIMNEY	OWNERSHIP, ETC.
tar-paper shack	none	stove pipe	owner of house
frame house	logs	brick	renter (amt.)
log cabin	stone		squatter
rehab. house	cement		own land
		PORCH	allot. land
		earth	U.S. land
STORIES	ROOF	stone	white man's land
attic	tar paper	flags	Meth. church land
upstairs	tin	platform	tax delinquent
downstairs	shingle	roofed	insurance
cellar	roofing	screened	mortgage

ROOMS

On mimeograph allow space for the following information for six rooms—for living-room, dining-room, kitchen, and three bedrooms.

USE OF ROOM	CEILING	FULL WINDOWS	HALF WINDOWS
	unfinished	number	number
DIMENSIONS	newspaper	total broken	total broken
height	lumber	shade, etc.	shade, etc.
width	plaster	adjustable	adjustable
length	wall paper	screen	screen
	painted		
INSIDE DOORS		LESS HALF	OUTSIDE DOORS
number	WALLS	WINDOWS	rough lumber
mere openings	unfinished	number	tar paper
cloth hangings	newspaper	total broken	panelled
rough lumber	lumber	shade, etc.	screen door
panelled	plaster	adjustable	
	wall paper	screen	FLOORS
	painted		dirt
			wood

Would you like to leave this home?

Would you like to move into a rehabilitation house, one of those fine new houses the Indian Bureau built for the Indians?

II. THE FAMILIES

PERSONAL HISTORY OF FATHER AND MOTHER

Father (Record same information for mother.)

AGE

BIRTHPLACE	LANGUAGES
reservation	spoken
White Earth	Chippewa
other Chippewa	English
non-Chippewa	understood
white community	Chippewa
	English

EDUCATION
last grade attended
high school 1, 2, 3, 4 yrs.
schools attended (names)
trade learnt

RELIGION
Midē wiwin
Protestant denomination
Catholic

PRESENT MARRIAGE
common law
legal
church denomination

PREVIOUS MARRIAGES
(Record for each marriage)
common law
legal
church denomination
number
spouse dead
divorced
parted

EXPERIENCE OFF THE RESERVATION
never been off the reservation
less than 100 miles off reservation
St. Paul or/and Minneapolis
States bounding Minnesota
North Dakota
South Dakota
Iowa
Wisconsin
other states
Canada
Mexico
Europe

INSURANCE
life
accident

USE OF FRANCHISE
State Primary (June 20, 1938)
Referendum (June 18, 1938)

CHILDREN IN THE FAMILY
preschool (number)
elementary school
5th grade or below
6th grade or beyond
day school
number attending
boarding school
number attending
names of schools

SHELTERING HOMELESS CHILDREN
grandchildren
of legitimate birth
of illegitimate birth
legally adopted
adopted "Indian way"
other children
legally adopted
adopted "Indian way"

SOCIAL PROBLEMS
Why are there so many unmarried mothers on the reservation?
(Any unmarried mother in the home? How many children?)
(Check this information with some outside person.)

Why are there so many common-law marriages on the reservation?

What do you think can be done to eliminate drinking to intoxication among the Indians? (Any intoxication in the home? Father? Mother? Son? Daughter?) (Check this information with outside person.)

Just what do you think can be done to better social conditions on the White Earth Reservation? What would you want your tribal delegate to discuss at the next tribal council?

Check attendance at Sunday services with reliable outside person.

If possible interview all youth in family between ages of fifteen and twenty-one to discover their aspirations, plans for future, and problems.

III. LIVING CONDITIONS

HOUSEHOLD EQUIPMENT

KITCHEN UTENSILS
frying pans
roasters
kettles & pens
bread-mixing pans
bread tins
pie tins
coffee pot
tea pot
butcher knife
paring knife

TABLE SERVICE
plates
cups
saucers
dessert dishes
drinking glasses
knives
forks
vegetable dishes
platters
salt & pepper shakers

STORAGE PLACE
pantry
kitchen cabinet
cupboard
pegs on wall
table

HEATING & COOKING
APPARATUS
kitchen stove
   wood
   coal
   kerosene
   gasoline
   cooking
   baking
   heating
heaters
   kitchen stove
   "oil-drum"
   heater
outdoor fire
   tripod
   horizontal bar
   leaning stick
   grates
   discarded stove

TABLES
homemade
factory-made
writing table
bulrush mats

FUEL–WOOD
purchased
self-supplied

BEDS & BEDDING
bedsteads
   wooden
   homemade
   metal
cots
mattresses
   commercial
   feathers
   deer hair
   straw
comforters & blankets
   woolen
   cotton
   patched quilts

BEDS & BEDDING (CONT.)
pillows
  feathers
    chicken
    wild fowl
  deer hair
beds on floor

TABLECLOTH
cotton
linen
linoleum
oilcloth

CHAIRS
rockers
armchairs
chairs with backs
backless chairs
benches
boxes
cans

SLEEPING
ARRANGEMENTS
occupants of beds
  parents alone
  parents & children
    number in bed
  children alone
  number in bed
    both sexes
    age of each
sleeping-rooms
  number
  privacy–parents
  privacy–adolescents

RADIO
battery
electrical
in use
model
  console
  table
tubes
style

FACE TOWELS
number

SEWING MACHINE
own one
borrowed one
usable

TIME PIECE
watch
alarm clock
mantel
wall
sundial

ARTIFICIAL LIGHT
kerosene
gasoline
electric

RUGS
braided rags
braided bulrush
woven cat-tail
factory-made
  large
  small
linoleum
  large
  small

BED LINENS
sheets
  number
  commercial
  flour sacks
  quilt covers
pillow slips
  number
  commercial
  flour sacks

SUN SHELTER
branches
canvas
old cloth

MUSICAL INSTRUMENTS
Midē wiwin drum
Midē wiwin rattle
Chippewa flute
"pow-wow" drum
piano
organ
violin
banjo
ukelele
accordian
harmonica
drum
phonograph
others

STORAGE FACILITIES
foods
  outdoor caches
  under house
    cellar
    dugout
clothes, etc.
  inbuilt closets
  drawer chests
  dressers
  trunks
  open shelves
  pegs
  lines
  storage house
  attic

LAUNDRY APPARATUS
washing machines
  electric
  gasoline
  hand power
washboard
washtub
boiler
  commercial
  lard can
  dish pan
  pail
wringer

NEEDLECRAFT
table runners
doilies
lounging pillows
pillow slips
bedspreads

HOUSE PLANTS, ETC.
flowers
   garden
   wild
   artificial
potted plants

WALL DECORATIONS
enlarged photographs
assorted kodaks
colored prints
calendar
religious articles
guns
taxidermic products

CANNING
qts. in 1937

READING MATTER
Reference books
encyclopedias
books of fiction
text books
newspapers (names)
subscriber
   daily
   weekly
   Sunday
purchaser
   daily
   weekly
   Sunday
periodicals
subscriber (titles)
purchaser (titles)
library facilities

ANIMALS
dog
   hunting
   pet
cat
chickens
chicks
cow
calf
horse
other

DRINKING WATER
flowing spring
river
lake
well
no. using
distance
piped–house

WATER FOR WASHING
cistern
catch rain
lake, river
melted snow
well

YARD
dirt
wild grass
   cut
   uncut
lawn
fenced in
flower beds

TOILET FACILITIES
brush arbor
boards–no door
outdoor house
indoor

GARDENS
size
cost of plowing

GARDENS (CONT.)
contents
   vegetables (names)
   fruit trees (names)
   berries (names)
use
   immediate
   canning
   drying
   storing

INCOME
monthly income
source
   W.P.A.
   N.Y.A.
   C.C.C.–I.D.
   Div. of Roads–I.S.
   vet. pension
   O.A.A.
   private efforts

OTHER CHIPPEWA TRAITS
beadwork
moccasins
buckskin suits
Midē wiwin drum
Midē wiwin rattle
birch-bark articles
   baskets
   trays
   makuks
medicinal herbs
tanning hides
collecting birch bark
gathering wild rice
   home consumption
   sale
making maple sugar
   home consumption
   sale
wigwam, tipi
   bark
   blankets
   canvas
   use
      as dwelling
      for sleeping

MONEY ON DEPOSIT
bank
U.S. Post Office
with other person

PRESERVING MEAT
smoking
    Chippewa way
    in box
    smoke house
    smoke salt
    liquid smoke
use
    immediate
    storage

PRESERVING FISH
smoking
    Chippewa way
    in box
    smoke house
use
    immediate
    storage

GENERAL IMPRESSION
OF HOME
cleanliness and order
    best possible
    tolerable
    filthy
attractiveness
    glad to eat here
    only if very hungry
    only if starving

Appendix B

MAPS OF THE WHITE EARTH RESERVATION OF THE
MINNESOTA CHIPPEWA RESERVATIONS

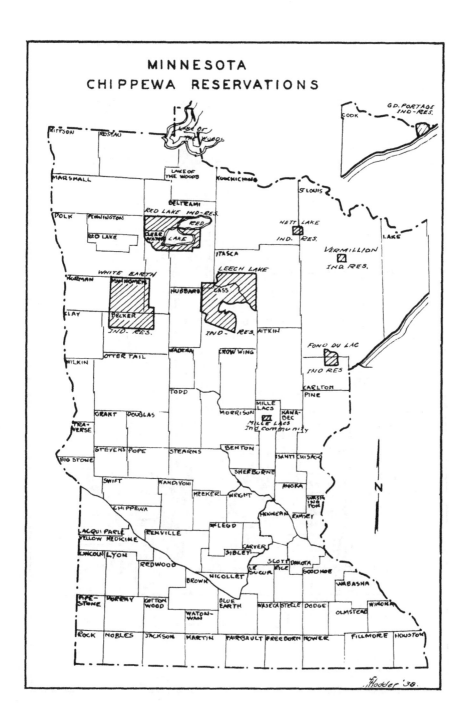

MINNESOTA
CHIPPEWA RESERVATIONS

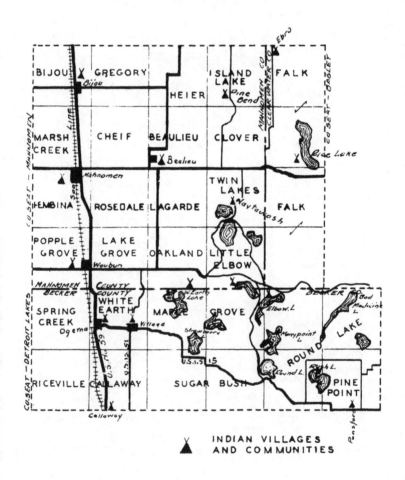

WHITE EARTH INDIAN RESERVATION

Scale of Miles

△ INDIAN VILLAGES AND COMMUNITIES

Appendix C

SUMMARY TABULATIONS OF HOUSING CONDITIONS OF
ONE HUNDRED FIFTY CHIPPEWA INDIAN FAMILIES ON THE
WHITE EARTH RESERVATION OF MINNESOTA IN 1938

HOUSING CONDITIONS	SEVENTY-ONE TAR-PAPER SHACK FAMILIES	SEVENTY-ONE FRAME-HOUSE FAMILIES	EIGHT U.S. REHABILITATION-HOUSE FAMILIES	ALL TYPES
Wigwams owned and occupied	2	–	–	2
Size of house				
One room	36	2	–	38
Two rooms	22	21	1	44
Three rooms	12	21	6	39
Four rooms	1	11	1	13
Five rooms	–	7	–	7
Six rooms or more	–	9	–	9
Total	71	71	8	150
Total cubic feet of air space				
Smallest house	630	720	2880	
Largest house	5940	10368	5040	
Roofing				
Tar paper	65	20	–	85
Wooden shingles	6	51	8	65
Total	71	71	8	150
Foundation				
none	67	38	–	105
Stone	–	10	–	10
Log	4	–	–	4
Cement	–	23	8	31
Total	71	71	8	150
Chimney				
Stove pipe	66	31	–	97
Brick	5	44	8	57
Total	71	75*	8	154

*Four houses had both types of chimneys.

HOUSING CONDITIONS	SEVENTY-ONE TAR-PAPER SHACK FAMILIES	SEVENTY-ONE FRAME-HOUSE FAMILIES	EIGHT U.S. REHABILITATION-HOUSE FAMILIES	ALL TYPES
Porches				
None, flat stones, or boards	12	5	–	17
One- or two-step platforms without roof	58	49	–	107
One- or two-step platforms with roof	1	12	7	20
Screened	–	5	1	6
Total	71	71	8	150
Interior wall finishings of all rooms				
Unfinished	36	8	–	44
Rosin paper	39	31	–	70
Lumber	4	16	8	28
Composition board	–	2	–	2
Paint or whitewash	4	24	8	36
Plaster	1	19	–	20
Wall paper	–	1	–	1
Height of ceilings				
Five feet	2	–	–	2
Six feet	11	5	–	16
Seven feet	10	10	–	20
Eight feet	28	34	8	70
Nine feet	13	10	–	23
Ten feet or more	7	12	–	19
Total	71	71	8	150
Number of windows				
Broken ones	17	22	–	39
Less than half-size	47	14	–	61
Half-size	104	41	6	151
Full-size	162	376	47	585
Number of doors				
Open passage ways	23	21	–	44
Cloth hangings	2	1	–	3
Rough lumber	51	19	–	70
Panelled	37	129	19	185
Screens				
All outside doors	36	55	8	99
No windows	10	1	–	11
Some windows	2	–	–	2
All windows	59	70	8	137

HOUSING CONDITIONS	SEVENTY-ONE TAR-PAPER SHACK FAMILIES	SEVENTY-ONE FRAME-HOUSE FAMILIES	EIGHT U.S. REHABILITATION-HOUSE FAMILIES	ALL TYPES
Ownership of homes	55	26	–	81
Attitude toward present location of homes				
Unwilling to leave homes	52	22	8	82
Willing to move	7	40	–	47
Undecided	12	9	–	21
Total	71	71	8	150

Appendix D

SUMMARY TABULATIONS DESCRIPTIVE OF
ONE HUNDRED FIFTY CHIPPEWA INDIAN FAMILIES
ON THE WHITE EARTH RESERVATION
OF MINNESOTA IN 1938

ITEMS	SEVENTY-ONE TAR-PAPER SHACK FAMILIES	SEVENTY-ONE FRAME-HOUSE FAMILIES	EIGHT U.S. REHABILITATION-HOUSE FAMILIES	ALL CASES
PARENTS IN THE HOMES				
Fathers	61	66	6	133
Mothers	70	68	8	146
Total	131	134	14	279
AGE GROUP OF PARENTS				
First generation (born 1839–1872)	28	18	–	46
Second generation (born 1871–1905)	68	76	9	153
Third generation (born since 1904)	35	40	5	80
Total	131	134	14	279
MARITAL STATUS OF PARENTS				
Present marriages				
Common-law marriages	19	2	1	22
Legal marriages	15	16	2	33
Marriages in Protestant churches	11	6	2	19
Marriages in the Catholic church	26	47	3	76
Total	71	71	8	150

ITEMS	SEVENTY-ONE TAR-PAPER SHACK FAMILIES	SEVENTY-ONE FRAME-HOUSE FAMILIES	EIGHT U.S. REHABILITATION-HOUSE FAMILIES	ALL CASES
Mixed marriages				
Midē wiwin and				
Catholic	3	–	–	3
Midē wiwin and				
Protestant	3	–	–	3
Catholic and				
Protestant	16	11	–	27
Total	22	11	–	33
Ancestry of parents				
Indian tribe other				
than Chippewa				
Fathers	3	–	–	3
Mothers	–	–	–	–
European				
Fathers	4	5	–	9
Mothers	4	11	–	15
Chippewa				
Fathers	54	61	6	121
Mothers	66	57	8	131
Total	131	134	14	279
Separation and divorce				
Separation	7	3	1	11
Divorce	2	5	–	7
Total	9	8	1	18
Previous marriages				
One previous				
marriage				
Fathers	15	7	–	22
Mothers	13	14	1	28
Two previous				
marriages				
Fathers	3	2	1	6
Mothers	1	–	–	1
Three previous				
marriages				
Fathers	2	1	–	3
Mothers	2	–	–	2
Total	36	24	2	62

ITEMS	SEVENTY-ONE TAR-PAPER SHACK FAMILIES	SEVENTY-ONE FRAME-HOUSE FAMILIES	EIGHT U.S. REHABILITATION-HOUSE FAMILIES	ALL CASES
FAMILY COMPOSITION AND CHILDREN IN THE HOMES				
Size of families				
Mean for children	3.79	3.43	3.20	3.47
Mean for all persons in the home	5.83	5.47	4.20	5.17
The children in the family				
Preschool children	46	39	5	90
Children of school age	110	103	11	224
Total	156	142	16	314
Children in boarding schools				
Mission schools	11	7	–	18
U.S. Government schools	17	11	–	28
Total	28	18	–	46
Care of homeless children				
Homes sheltering children, non-members of family	25	34	5	64
Number of children of legitimate birth				
Both parents dead	16	13	1	30
One parent dead	3	7	–	10
Number of children born out of wedlock	7	22	9	38
Total	26	42	10	78
RETENTION OF CHIPPEWA LANGUAGE				
Chippewa only language spoken				
Fathers	6	2	–	8
Mothers	8	6	–	14
Total	14	8	–	22
Chippewa and English				
Fathers	43	31	4	78
Mothers	49	34	3	86
Total	92	65	7	164

ITEMS	SEVENTY-ONE TAR-PAPER SHACK FAMILIES	SEVENTY-ONE FRAME-HOUSE FAMILIES	EIGHT U.S. REHABILITATION-HOUSE FAMILIES	ALL CASES
Chippewa understood but not spoken				
Fathers	4	4	–	8
Mothers	3	8	2	13
Total	7	12	2	21
Grand total	113	85	9	207
EDUCATIONAL OPPORTUNITIES OF PARENTS				
Formal education of parents				
Illiterate				
Fathers	19	13	–	32
Mothers	18	9	–	27
Total	37	22	–	59
Attended grades between first and eighth				
Fathers	25	26	2	53
Mothers	26	25	2	53
Total	51	51	4	106
Entered eighth grade				
Fathers	9	14	3	26
Mothers	17	15	4	36
Total	26	29	7	62
Spent some time in high school				
Fathers	3	12	1	16
Mothers	14	20	2	36
Total	17	32	3	52
Grand total	131	134	14	279
Attendance at boarding school				
Fathers	43	47	5	95
Mothers	59	61	8	128
Total	102	108	13	223
Birthplace of parents				
Fathers				
White Earth Reservation	42	47	5	94
Other Chippewa reservation	6	5	1	12
In white community	13	14	–	27
Total	61	66	6	133

ITEMS	SEVENTY-ONE TAR-PAPER SHACK FAMILIES	SEVENTY-ONE FRAME-HOUSE FAMILIES	EIGHT U.S. REHABILITATION-HOUSE FAMILIES	ALL CASES
Birthplace of parents (cont.)				
Mothers				
White Earth				
Reservation	44	45	8	97
Other Chippewa				
reservation	13	6	–	19
In white community	13	17	–	30
Total	70	68	8	146
Grand total	131	134	14	279
EXPERIENCE OFF THE RESERVATION				
Travelled less than 100 miles off reservation				
Fathers	18	7	2	27
Mothers	35	27	3	65
Total	53	34	5	92
Never visited St. Paul or Minneapolis				
Fathers	43	35	2	80
Mothers	.52	45	5	102
Total	95	80	7	182
Trip into states bounding Minnesota				
Fathers	34	69	6	109
Mothers	42	49	4	95
Total	76	118	10	204
World War service abroad				
Fathers	1	4	–	5
Member of Indian baseball team				
Fathers	–	3	–	3
RELIGIOUS AFFILIATION OF PARENTS				
Midē wiwin				
Fathers	7	–	–	7
Mothers	8	–	–	8
Total	15	–	–	15
Catholic				
Fathers	32	49	3	84
Mothers	39	58	5	102
Total	71	107	8	186

ITEMS	SEVENTY-ONE TAR-PAPER SHACK FAMILIES	SEVENTY-ONE FRAME-HOUSE FAMILIES	EIGHT U.S. REHABILITATION- HOUSE FAMILIES	ALL CASES
Protestant				
Fathers	23	14	3	40
Mothers	24	11	3	38
Total	47	25	6	78

POLITICAL EXPRESSION OF PARENT

Voting

Referendum tribal vote, June 18, 1938

Fathers	42	43	5	90
Mothers	32	45	6	83
Total	74	88	11	173

State Primary Election, June 20, 1938

Fathers	45	49	6	100
Mothers	38	43	8	89
Total	83	92	14	189

SOCIAL PROBLEMS OF THE FAMILIES

Unmarried mothers

With one child	5	9	–	14
With two children	1	3	2	6
With three children	–	1	1	2
With four children	–	1	–	1
Total	6	14	3	23

Total number of children born out of wedlock	7	22	7	36

Drinking to excess

Both parents	4	4	–	8
Both parents and adolescent youth	1	1	–	2
One parent and adolescent youth	4	2	–	6
Father only	6	9	–	15
Mother only	1	2	–	3
Adolescent youth only	–	2	2	4
Total	16	20	2	38

ITEMS	SEVENTY-ONE TAR-PAPER SHACK FAMILIES	SEVENTY-ONE FRAME-HOUSE FAMILIES	EIGHT U.S. REHABILITATION-HOUSE FAMILIES	ALL CASES
The problem of youth Homes with				
adolescent youth	24	38	2	64
Youth with problems Unmarried mothers	6	14	3	23
Drinking to excess				
Young men	1	3	–	4
Young women	4	2	2	8
Total	11	19	5	35

Appendix E

SUMMARY TABULATIONS OF LIVING CONDITIONS
OF ONE HUNDRED FIFTY CHIPPEWA INDIAN FAMILIES
ON THE WHITE EARTH RESERVATION
OF MINNESOTA IN 1938

LIVING CONDITIONS INCLUDING SOME PHASES OF ECONOMIC LIFE	SEVENTY-ONE TAR-PAPER SHACK FAMILIES	SEVENTY-ONE FRAME-HOUSE FAMILIES	EIGHT U.S. REHABILITATION-HOUSE FAMILIES	ALL ITEMS
SIZE AND USE OF ROOMS				
Mean cubic feet of air space per person per room	7.08	4.17	35.12	
Use of rooms				
Homes with rooms used exclusively as:				
Living-room	–	14	2	16
Dining-room	–	3	–	3
Kitchen	9	17	–	26
Bedroom	21	45	6	72
Rooms serving two purposes				
Bedroom kitchen	3	2	–	5
Bedroom living-room	15	36	3	54
Dining-room kitchen	15	43	6	64
Living-room dining-room	1	5	–	6
Rooms serving three purposes				
Living-room dining-room bedroom	7	4	–	11
Living-room dining-room kitchen	8	6	2	16

LIVING CONDITIONS INCLUDING SOME PHASES OF ECONOMIC LIFE	SEVENTY-ONE TAR-PAPER SHACK FAMILIES	SEVENTY-ONE FRAME-HOUSE FAMILIES	EIGHT U.S. REHABILITATION- HOUSE FAMILIES	ALL ITEMS
Use of rooms (cont.)				
Rooms serving four purposes				
Living-room dining-room bedroom kitchen	37	2	–	39
Homes without private bedrooms for parents	34	20	1	55
HOUSEHOLD EQUIPMENT				
Beds and bedding (total number)				
Families making beds on floor	14	9	–	23
Mattresses				
Cotton (factory-made)	79	143	18	240
Feather	64	63	5	132
Deer-hair	3	2	–	5
Straw	5	–	–	5
Woolen coverings	38	128	6	172
Cotton coverings	269	395	49	713
Beds and bedding (mean number per family)				
Beds	2.6	2.9	2.4	
Mattresses	2.9	2.8	2.8	
Pillows	3.3	3.4	5.5	
Woolen coverings	.5	1.8	.7	
Cotton coverings	3.8	5.6	6.1	
Bed linens				
No sheets	15	2	1	18
Fewer than six sheets	54	60	4	118
No pillow slips	5	2	1	8
Fewer than six pillow slips	47	34	2	83
Face towels				
None	1	–	–	1
Fewer than six	57	26	3	86

LIVING CONDITIONS INCLUDING SOME PHASES OF ECONOMIC LIFE	SEVENTY-ONE TAR-PAPER SHACK FAMILIES	SEVENTY-ONE FRAME-HOUSE FAMILIES	EIGHT U.S. REHABILITATION-HOUSE FAMILIES	ALL ITEMS
Tableclothes				
None	11	7	1	19
Oilcloth	59	61	4	124
Cloth cover	2	6	3	11
Linoleum	2	–	–	2
Kitchen utensils (families not having any)				
Frying pans	10	19	2	31
Roaster	53	37	4	94
Kettles or cooking pans	2	–	–	2
Coffee pots	5	2	–	7
Tea pots	25	36	1	62
Tea kettles	26	13	2	41
Bread-mixing pan or dish pan	26	17	3	46
Bread tins	12	7	1	20
Pie tins	18	7	–	25
Butcher knives	1	1	–	2
Paring knives	31	27	3	61
Water pail	2	–	–	2
Table service (families not having any)				
Saucers	25	9	1	35
Dessert dishes	44	26	2	72
Vegetable dishes	25	16	2	43
Platters	28	14	1	43
Salt and pepper shakers	5	3	2	10
Water glasses	15	12	–	27
Storage place for kitchen utensils and table service (families without any)				
Pantries	70	69	–	139
Cabinets or cupboards	3	3	–	6
Cooking over outdoor fires				
Traditional way	40	22	1	63
Under grates	20	10	1	31

LIVING CONDITIONS INCLUDING SOME PHASES OF ECONOMIC LIFE	SEVENTY-ONE TAR-PAPER SHACK FAMILIES	SEVENTY-ONE FRAME-HOUSE FAMILIES	EIGHT U.S. REHABILITATION- HOUSE FAMILIES	ALL ITEMS
Heating facilities				
Kitchen stoves only	38	19	1	58
Heaters	33	52	7	92
Furnaces	–	2	–	2
Fuel				
Families				
gathering own wood	54	46	6	106
Families buying wood	17	25	2	44
Tables				
Homemade	42	28	1	71
Factory-made	29	43	7	79
Writing desks or tables	3	12	–	15
Chairs				
None	16	8	–	24
Rockers or arm-chairs	27	49	5	81
Backless chairs	28	21	–	49
Benches	45	38	1	84
Laundry apparatus				
Washing machines	17	24	3	44
No wash boards	2	–	–	2
No wash tubs	1	–	–	1
Sewing machines (owners)	35	42	3	80
Artificial light				
Kerosene lamps	72	62	8	142
Electric lights	–	9	–	9
Telling time				
No time piece	4	–	–	4
Watch	1	4	–	5
Alarm clock	60	61	7	128
Mantel clocks	5	5	–	10
Wall clocks	–	3	–	3
STORAGE FACILITIES				
Storage of foods				
Dug-out under house	25	43	8	76
Cellars	–	4	–	4

LIVING CONDITIONS INCLUDING SOME PHASES OF ECONOMIC LIFE	SEVENTY-ONE TAR-PAPER SHACK FAMILIES	SEVENTY-ONE FRAME-HOUSE FAMILIES	EIGHT U.S. REHABILITATION-HOUSE FAMILIES	ALL ITEMS
Storage of clothes and other effects				
Lines strung across corners	39	29	1	69
Pegs driven into walls	51	53	1	105
Inbuilt clothes closets	8	15	8	31
Trunks	42	50	5	97
Dressers	30	52	5	87
Drawer chests	9	13	–	22
Open shelves	24	37	–	61
Storage houses	17	18	3	38
Attics	6	22	5	33
EXPRESSIONS OF PERSONALITY				
Interior decoration of homes				
Articles of Chippewa culture	37	19	2	58
Flowers and plants				
Wild	–	4	–	4
Garden	12	15	2	29
Potted	7	12	1	20
Artificial	3	6	–	9
Needlecraft	23	32	4	59
Lounging pillows	8	16	3	27
Homemade braided rugs	35	38	6	79
Enlarged photographs	27	38	3	68
Framed snapshots	21	29	3	53
Calendars	69	65	7	141
Crucifix, statue, print of Saint	20	41	5	66
Taxidermic products	14	7	–	21
Guns	34	33	1	68
Music instruments				
Midē wiwin drum	2	–	–	2
"Pow-wow" drum	1	–	–	1
Shaman's drum	1	–	–	1
Shaman's rattle	2	–	–	2
Pianos	–	2	–	2
Organs	–	2	–	2
Guitars	3	6	1	10
Harmonicas	1	2	–	3
Ukulele	1	2	–	3
Violin	1	1	–	2

LIVING CONDITIONS INCLUDING SOME PHASES OF ECONOMIC LIFE	SEVENTY-ONE TAR-PAPER SHACK FAMILIES	SEVENTY-ONE FRAME-HOUSE FAMILIES	EIGHT U.S. REHABILITATION- HOUSE FAMILIES	ALL ITEMS
Music instruments (cont.)				
Banjo	2	1	–	3
Accordion	1	–	–	1
Radios				
Families owning one	22	46	4	72
Radios with dead batteries	12	13	–	25
Phonographs	3	4	–	7
Rugs				
Traditional bulrush mats	8	–	–	8
Braided rag rugs of six or eight ply	35	38	6	79
Small factory- woven rugs	3	5	2	10
Large factory- woven rugs	–	7	–	7
Small linoleum rugs	8	10	2	20
Large linoleum rugs	14	26	3	43
Reading matter in homes				
Reference books or books of fiction	11	17	3	31
Set of encyclopedias	1	1	–	2
Text books	9	7	–	16
Purchased Sunday papers	43	45	5	93
Subscribed for daily paper	2	6	2	10
Subscribed for periodical	12	17	2	31
Purchased periodical regularly	6	9	–	15
Yard				
Lawns	3	25	4	32
Flower beds	17	13	7	37
Fences about yards	17	36	3	56
Sun shelters				
Traditional type	4	–	–	4
Canvas covered ones	4	1	–	5

LIVING CONDITIONS INCLUDING SOME PHASES OF ECONOMIC LIFE	SEVENTY-ONE TAR-PAPER SHACK FAMILIES	SEVENTY-ONE FRAME-HOUSE FAMILIES	EIGHT U.S. REHABILITATION-HOUSE FAMILIES	ALL ITEMS
PRIVATE UTILITIES				
Drinking water				
Flowing springs	12	3	–	15
River water	1	1	–	2
Well water	68	67	8	143
Toilet facilities				
No privies	11	3	–	14
Planks about a seat	9	6	–	15
Privies with doors	51	62	–	113
Well-constructed sanitary toilets	–	–	8	–
Indoor toilets	–	–	–	–
ECONOMIC RESOURCES				
Income				
Families drawing U.S. Government checks	70	70	8	148
W.P.A	46	48	8	102
C.C.C.–I.D.	9	3	–	12
I.S. Div. of Roads	–	5	–	5
Pensions–World War veterans	2	1	–	3
Pensions–widows of World War veterans	2	2	–	4
Social Security Act (and State of Minnesota)				
Old age assistance (persons)	23	9	1	33
Direct county relief	1	–	–	1
Self-supporting (dairying)	–	1	–	1
Unpaid bills				
Grocery	41	42	7	90
Clothing	3	7	–	10
Automobiles, pickups, truck	13	16	–	29
Stoves	3	12	2	17
Radios	11	15	2	28
Sewing machines	1	2	–	3
Washing machines	6	8	2	16
Other bills	12	12	2	26

LIVING CONDITIONS INCLUDING SOME PHASES OF ECONOMIC LIFE	SEVENTY-ONE TAR-PAPER SHACK FAMILIES	SEVENTY-ONE FRAME-HOUSE FAMILIES	EIGHT U.S. REHABILITATION-HOUSE FAMILIES	ALL ITEMS
Families with gardens	61	63	7	131
Planted for storing or preserving	41	43	6	90
Canning of food Total number of families in fall of 1937	43	66	8	117
From 200 to 500 quarts	12	17	2	31
Raising berries for family use	3	5	1	9
Domesticated animals				
Dogs	37	42	6	85
Cats	35	39	5	79
Chickens	5	9	2	16
Cows	8	8	2	18
Providing food of the Chippewa pattern Wild rice (gathered in 1937)	35	8	–	43
Maple sugar (made in 1937)	5	2	–	7
Dried and smoked fish	12	3	–	15
Dried and smoked meat	11	3	–	14

Appendix F

Wigwam (Note birch-bark rolls, cloth coverings, and stove-pipe chimney.)

One-room tar-paper shack (Note homemade frames for doors and windows, panelled door, platform porch, stove for outdoor cooking.)

Four-room frame house largely overlaid with tar paper (Note types of windows, method of catching rain water, lean-to, yard.)

Backyard with garage, wood pile, privy (Note homemade doors.)

Two-room tar-paper shack and log cabin combined (Note factory-made frames for doors and windows, screened door and windows, pump, barn, chicken coop.)

Two-room frame house and tar-paper lean-to combined (Note chimneys of stove pipe and of brick, attic window, yard of uncut grass.)

Four-room frame house (Note factory-made door and window frames, screened door and windows, window shades, garden in foreground.)

Four-room U.S. rehabilitation house (Note roofed porch, cement foundation, pump and sanitary well construction.)

Literature Cited

A Housing Program for the United States, A Report Prepared for the National Association of Housing Officials. Chicago, Public Administrative Service, 1935.

Annual Extension Report for the Consolidated Chippewa Agency for 1937. Duluth, Consolidated Chippewa Agency, 1937. (Manuscript).

Armstrong, Benj. G.: *Early Life among the Indians.* Ashland, A. W. Bowron, 1892.

"Basic Principles of Healthful Housing." *American Journal of Public Health,* 28: March, 1938.

Bushnell, David I.: *Ojibway Habitations and Other Structures.* Washington, Government Printing Office, 1919. (In Annual Report of the Smithsonian Institution for the year ending June 30, 1917).

———. *Native Villages and Village Sites East of the Mississippi.* Washington, Government Printing Office, 1919. (U.S. Bureau of American Ethnology Bulletin 69).

Carlson, E. J.: *Annual Forestry and Grazing Report for the Fiscal Year of 1937.* Duluth, Consolidated Chippewa Agency, 1937. (Manuscript).

1937 Census of the White Earth Reservation. 1938 Supplemental Census and Addition Roll. 1938 Deduction Roll. Duluth, Consolidated Chippewa Agency, 1938.

Constitution and By-laws of the Minnesota Chippewa. Washington, Government Printing Office, 1936.

Copway, George: *The Traditional History and Characteristic Sketches of the Ojibway Nation.* Boston, Benj. B. Mussey & Co., 1851.

Corporate Charter of the Minnesota Chippewa Tribe of the Consolidated Chippewa Agency. Washington, Government Printing Office, 1938.

Densmore, Frances: *Chippewa Customs.* Washington, Government Printing Office, 1929. (U.S. Bureau of American Ethnology Bulletin 86).

Gilfillan, Joseph A.: *The Ojibways in Minnesota.* St. Paul, Minnesota Historical Society, 1901. (In Collections of the Minnesota Historical Society, IX).

Hilger, Sister M. Inez: "In the Early Days of Wisconsin, An Amalgamation of Chippewa and European Cultures." *Wisconsin Archeologist,* 16:32–49, June, 1936.

——. "Chippewa Interpretation of Natural Phenomena." *Scientific Monthly,* 45:178–179, August, 1937.

——. "Some Phases of Chippewa Material Culture." *Anthropos,* 32 [1937], 780–782.

Hodge, Frederick Webb: *Handbook of American Indians North of Mexico.* Washington, Government Printing Office, 1907. (U.S. Bureau of American Ethnology Bulletin 30, Part 1).

Hoffman, W. J.: *The Midé wiwin or "Grand Medicine Society" of the Ojibwa.* Washington, Government Printing Office, 1891. (In Seventh Annual Report of the U.S. Bureau of Ethnology, 1885–1886).

Indian Emergency Conservation Program, April 1. 1937 to June 30, 1938. Duluth, Consolidated Chippewa Agency. (Manuscript).

Kappler, Charles J.: (ed.) *Indian Affairs: Laws and Treaties.* Washington, Government Printing Office, I, 1903; II, 1903; III, 1913; IV, 1929.

Kellogg, Louise Phelps: (ed.) *Early Narratives of the Northwest, 1634–1699.* New York, Charles Scribner's Sons, 1917.

Kinney, Jay P.: *A Continent Lost–A Civilization Won, Indian Land Tenure in America.* Baltimore, Johns Hopkins Press, 1937.

Land records. Duluth, Consolidated Chippewa Agency, 1938.

Lists Showing the Degree of Indian Blood of Certain Persons Holding Land upon the White Earth Reservation in Minnesota and a List Showing the Date of Certain Persons Who Held Land upon Such Reservation. Washington, Government Printing Office, 1911.

McKinsey, Shirley: *Report of 1937–1938 Based on a Survey of the Six Chippewa Reservations under the Consolidated Chippewa Agency.* Duluth, Consolidated Chippewa Agency, 1938. (Manuscript).

Oliphant, Laurence: *Minnesota and the Far West.* Edinburgh and London, William Blackwood & Sons, 1855.

Pierz, Franz: *Die Indianer in Nord-Amerika, ihre Lebensweise, Sitten, Gebrauche, etc.* St. Louis, Franz Saler & Co., 1855.

Report of January 19, 1935, of the Commissioner of the U.S. Bureau of Indian Affairs to the U.S. Secretary of the Interior. (Manuscript).

Skinner, Alanson: *Notes on the Eastern Cree and Northern Saulteaux.* New York, American Museum of Natural History, 1911. (Anthropological Papers of the American Museum of Natural History, IX, Part 1).

Social and Economic Survey of 1934 of the Consolidated Chippewa Agency. Washington, U.S. Bureau of Indian Affairs. (Manuscript).

State of Minnesota Old Age Assistance Act, Adopted by Special Session of the Legislature of 1935–1936, Amended by Regular Session of the Legislature of 1937, and Including Other Laws Pertaining to Old Age Assistance Passed by 1937 Special Session of the Legislature. St. Paul, State Board of Control, 1937.

State of Minnesota Aid to Dependent Children Act, Adopted by the Legislature of 1937. St. Paul, State Board of Control, 1937.

Survey of Conditions of the Indians of the United States, Covering Hearings of 1933 before a Subcommittee of Indian Affairs of the United States Senate, Seventy-third Congress. Washington, Government Printing Office, 1934.

Tribal Roll of the Minnesota Chippewa Indians. Duluth, Consolidated Chippewa Agency, 1938.

U.S. House Executive Documents. No. 247, 51st Congress, 1st Session.

U.S. Statutes at Large. Vol. 43, Ch. 233.

U.S. Statutes at Large. Vol. 48, Ch. 147.

Warren, William: *History of the Ojibways.* St. Paul, Minnesota Historical Society, 1885. (In Collections of the Minnesota Historical Society, V).

Winchell, N. H.: (ed.) *The Aborigines of Minnesota, A Report Based on the Collection of Jacob V. Brower, and on the Field Surveys and Notes of Alfred J. Hill and Theodore H. Lewis.* St. Paul, Minnesota Historical Society, 1911.

Wissler, Clark: *The American Indian, An Introduction to the Anthropology of the New World.* New York, Oxford University Press, American Branch, 1922.

Index

185